THE
REFERENCE
SHELF

IMMIGRATION

Edited by ROBERT EMMET LONG

THE REFERENCE SHELF

Volume 68 Number 1

THE H. W. WILSON COMPANY

New York   Dublin   1996

THE REFERENCE SHELF

The books in this series contain reprints of articles, excerpts from books, addresses on current issues, and studies of social trends in the United States and other countries. There are six numbers to a volume, all of which are usually published in a single calendar year. Numbers one through five devote themselves to a single subject, give background information and discussion from various points of view, concluding with a comprehensive bibliography that contains books, pamphlets and abstracts of additional articles on the subject. The final number is a collection of recent speeches. This number also contains a subject index to the entire Reference Shelf volume. Books in the series may be purchased individually or on subscription.

Library of Congress Cataloging-in-Publication Data

Immigration / edited by Robert Emmet Long.
    p.   cm. — (Reference shelf ; v. 68, no. 1)
    Includes bibliographical references.
    ISBN 0-8242-0886-2
    1. United States—Emigration and immigration. 2. United States—Emigration and immigration—Government policy. 3. Illegal aliens—United States. I. Long, Robert Emmet. II. Series.
JV6465.I47   1996
325.73—dc20   95-52085
                                      CIP

Cover: People stand on line at the Immigration and Naturalization Service desk. *Photo:* Bettmann Newsphotos

Printed in the United States of America

CONTENTS

IV. THE IMMIGRATION POLICY DEBATE

PREFACE

During the 1990s immigration into the United States has been soaring, and with it has come a heated controversy over the nation's immigration policy, which critics charge is in need of radical and immediate overhaul. Illegal immigration in particular has angered many groups, including conservatives, who are demanding that the border between Mexico and the U.S. be sealed. The number of illegal immigrants in this country is difficult to fix precisely but it may be as high as four million and all are eligible for educational, medical, and welfare benefits. At a time when American businesses are downsizing and a sense of anxiety is often felt about the nation's future, illegal immigrants have come under heavy fire. The issue of the illegals has already entered American politics; it was a factor in Pete Wilson's reelection as governor of California, and it seems bound to be an issue in the presidential election in 1996. This compilation brings together many informative and provocative articles that make the immigration issue clearer in its many aspects.

Debate over immigration and immigration policy is not new to the nation's history. Immigration—mainly from Germany and Ireland—swelled the United States' population from four million in 1790 to thirty-two million in 1860. Predictably, anti-immigrant feeling rose with the flood of immigrants and in this period the anti-Catholic, anti-foreign political party, the Know-Nothings, was born. Between the Civil War and the end of the century, some fourteen million immigrants arrived, and already eighteen million by 1930, many from Russia, Poland, Italy, and eastern Europe.

From time to time, Congress jarred legislation to control the flow of immigration. An 1882 law excluded Chinese from entry. In 1924, the Johnson-Reed Act set national quotas that were followed for many years, that gave half of all places to British residents, and excluded Asians altogether. The Immigration Act of 1965 reduced the proportion of immigrants from Europe to 10 percent and allowed the bulk of new immigrants to come from Asia and the Western Hemisphere. Then came the Vietnam influx, and the Refugee Act of 1980, which brought the Cuban refugees. The Simpson-Mazzoli Act of 1986 provided amnesty for pre-1982 illegal immigrants. Today, the country stands at the threshold of new legislation that will almost certainly have profound effects on the demographics of the U.S. in the 21st century.

Section One is devoted to the asylum seekers who have continued to arrive in record numbers from Asia and from Castro's Cuba. One article discusses the Clinton administration's decision to intercept Cuban "rafters" at sea and detain them indefinitely at Guantanamo Bay, a way of easing the almost unmanageable burden of refugees in Florida. Another article examines both the earlier refugees from Cuba, intransigent in their opposition to the Castro regime, and the newer generation of refugees who favor some kind of accommodation with their homeland. Other pieces in this section treat the Asian immigration experience that be harrowing and involve virtual bondage of immigrants to those who smuggled them into the country. Yet a piece on Koreans in New York City tells another story—of phenomenal success and relentless striving.

Nothing has stirred more controversy than the influx of illegals across the Mexican border—the subject of Section Two. The opening piece in this section describes the conditions—the high proportion of young men in Mexican society and the dearth of jobs for them—that make illegal border crossings widespread and almost inevitable. As another piece points out, the Mexican authorities do not do all they might do to suppress such crossings, since those who leave ease the problem of unemployment and the remittances they send back to their families add significantly to the country's economy. In an address, Republican presidential aspirant Patrick Buchanan demands an end to illegal entry into the U.S. but in the next article he is attacked for his inflammatory rhetoric and xenophobic attitudes. The final article refers to previous historical periods in which high rates of immigration produced a backlash of resentment and pronounced hostility.

Proposition 187 in California, with which Section Three is concerned, is a benchmark in the immigration debate. Articles in this section discuss the grassroots movement behind the 1994 referendum, which bars illegal immigrants from receiving welfare, education or health benefits. An address is included by California governor Pete Wilson, in which he announces that he is filing suit against the federal government for its failure to secure the nation's borders. Another piece offers a plan for dealing with the problem of immigration; and an article in the *New York Times* reports the view of New York City mayor Rudolph Giuliani that denying public schooling to children of illegals would create catastrophic social problems for New York and other large urban areas.

The final section is concerned with conflicting viewpoints in the immigration debate. Three of the section's articles deal with Peter Brimelow's controversial book, *Alien Nation*. The first two are reviews on the recent book which states the conservative case for slowing the pace of immigration, sealing the border between Mexico and the U.S., and terminating all benefits to illegal aliens. The following article from *New York* disagrees with Brimelow's views. Two closing articles consider immigration as an issue with the potential to affect United States' foreign policy.

The editor is indebted to the authors and publishers who have granted permission to reprint the materials in this collection. Thanks are also due to the staff of Penfield Library and State University of New York College at Oswego.

Robert Emmet Long

September 1995

I. REFUGEES FROM CUBA/NEW WAVE FROM ASIA

EDITOR'S INTRODUCTION

The articles in this section focus on two groups that have been frequently covered in the media—refugees from Cuba and immigrants, legal and illegal, from Asia. In the opening article, reprinted from *Time,* Nancy R. Gibbs reports on the Clinton administration's recent shift in policy regarding refugees arriving in makeshift boats and rafts from Cuba. They will now be intercepted and held in detention indefinitely at the U.S. naval base at Guantanamo Bay. Coming in such large numbers, they have overtaxed the resources of relief agencies in Florida, so that the state's governor, Lawton Chiles, has declared a state of emergency. In 1994, the cost of defraying costs of health care, social services, and law enforcement for the newcomers was estimated at $1 billion. A related article in *Dissent* by Román de la Campa examines successive waves of immigration from Cuba to the U.S., noting the differences between the 1960s refugees—largely upper-class and middle-class professionals displaced by Castro's coming to power, who have adamantly rejected any accommodation with his regime—and the more recent mainly working class generation of refugees, who incline to a more relaxed interchange with Cuba. The author concludes that it might be time to try again for some form of reconciliation with Castro.

Several articles that follow are concerned with the influx of illegal immigrants from Hong Kong, Taiwan, and mainland China, and with their condition after arriving in America. Melinda Liu's article from *Newsweek* concerns the incident in which a ship called the *Golden Venture* ran aground on New York's Rockaway Peninsula. Six of the passengers, part of a consignment of nearly three hundred Chinese being smuggled into America, died in their attempt to swim to shore. The incident, Liu notes, is part of a much larger pattern of trafficking in human beings that has become a multibillion-dollar business. Operatives known as "snakeheads" charge their clients anywhere from $30,000 to $50,000 for transportation from Asia to America, where they often become virtual slaves to those to whom they owe such a large debt. An article by Peter Kwong in *The Nation* explains the background conditions in China—poverty and wide-scale unemployment—that impels thousands of young people to embark on the risky and expensive course of illegal immigration.

A final piece, by Jeffrey Goldberg and reprinted from *New York,* calls attention to a group of immigrants from Korea, who have enjoyed good fortune in America through their determined effort to succeed. Goldberg refers to them as perhaps the "most instantly successful immigrant group in American history," but their remarkable success has come at a price. The parents have made extraordinary sacrifices to be able to send their children to the best colleges and to launch them in the well-paid professions. Moreover, a conflict of generations has developed in which the young, having moved away from the traditional values and prescribed behavior patterns of the parents, feel guilt for success brought about by the sacrifices of their parents.

DIRE STRAITS[1]

Looking for freedom and food, the Cuban refugees who hauled themselves desperately onto Floridian shores . . . told wild, hungry stories of how fellow countrymen tried to take advantage of the food shortage. They talked of condoms melted on top of pizzas and sold to the unsuspecting; of rag mops left in water to soften, then dried, cut up and served with egg on a sandwich; of apples that cost a month's wages. "We are like lambs," says Elvis Sierra Laborit, a bakery worker from Havana, who is not a rebellious man. "We will be eating grass soon." Even he realized it was time to go.

. . . U.S. officials tried their best to discourage Cubans from setting out on the treacherous 90-mile crossing to Florida. But it was clear that American threats stood little chance of prevailing over Cuba's hungers. By the time President Clinton went on television to reverse nearly thirty years of Cuban policy, he was characterizing the exodus as "a cold-blooded attempt to maintain the Castro grip on Cuba." Unwilling to be blackmailed by the threat

[1]Article by Nancy R. Gibbs, *Time* staff writer, from *Time* 144:28–32 Ag 29 '94. Copyright © 1994 by Time Inc. Reprinted with permission.

of a humanitarian disaster, Clinton revoked the special status Cuban refugees have long enjoyed, which guarantees them asylum if they reach U.S. shores.

Instead of the preferential treatment that has allowed Cubans to bypass the asylum process, the President announced on Friday [Aug. 26, 1994] that refugees trying to make it to the U.S. will now face indefinite detention while their cases are reviewed by immigration officials. . . . Clinton had imposed other stringencies on Cuba, including new limits on charter flights and an increase in anti-Castro radio broadcasts. Most important, Clinton pledged to cut off cash transfers from Cuban Americans to their relatives on the island—gifts that have been estimated to total $500 million a year.

Within hours of the announcement, Navy ships began collecting refugees intercepted by the Coast Guard and ferrying them to Guantánamo Bay Naval Station. The people of the U.S. "do not want to see Cuba dictate our immigration policy," Clinton declared. "They do not want to see Mr. Castro export his political and economic problems to the United States. We tried it that way once," he said, referring to the 1980 Mariel boatlift, which brought 125,000 refugees to America in five months. "It was wrong then, and it's wrong now, and I'm not going to let it happen again."

Under the new detention plan, refugees would be held at Guantánamo or other "safe havens." The legal key to their status is the Cuban Adjustment Act of 1966, a cold war loophole designed to help Cubans living illegally in the U.S. become citizens. The act allows the Attorney General "in his discretion" to guarantee permanent residency to Cuban refugees, but only after they have been in the U.S. for one year.

The wording of the statue and its twelve-month grace period enables the Clinton Administration, in effect, to turn the act upside-down, justifying the withholding of special considerations previously granted to Cubans and, in the process, reversing policy without actually having changed the law. In an afternoon briefing, Attorney General Janet Reno made it clear how she intends to use her discretionary powers. "Anybody who enters illegally," she said, "may be detained. The odds of ending up in Guantánamo are going to be very, very great. The odds of ending up in the U.S. are going to be very, very small."

Though the U.S. steps are designed to rob Castro of a safety vent to defuse unrest in his country, the number of Cubans taking to the sea did not immediately diminish in the wake of Clinton's pronouncements. On Friday, about 575 refugees arrived; Saturday brought another 861. Moreover, the President's stiffened economic sanctions will only increase the tensions that send Cubans dashing toward the beaches in the first place. At the same time, Castro's castaways must now swallow a humiliating demotion in status. The waning of superpower rivalry has weakened Cubans' claims to being fugitives from political oppression; instead they are now viewed simply as poor people trying to slip through the door to American prosperity—even as the U.S. anachronistically continues to treat Havana as it has since the late '50s and '60s: as a dangerous purveyor of subversion and Soviet expansionism.

The pressures on Castro at home have forced the Cuban leader to play a risky game. Castro's goal, argues a State Department official, "is to force us to negotiate the embargo." By threatening to swamp South Florida with another wave of refugees, Castro was gambling he could wring concessions out of the U.S. without destroying his own regime in the process. "What he's always good at is flipping things so his problem becomes someone else's," says the official. "This is his last card. He knows this is the one thing he can do to get our attention and inflict some measure of cost on us."

U.S. officials guess as many as three million of Cuba's eleven million citizens would flee if promised safe passage—an exodus that could be fatally humiliating to Castro but equally damaging to Clinton in Florida, an important re-election state. Having chided Castro for running a big prison, Clinton cannot very well tell him to keep the doors to the jail shut. But Floridians were adamant: they would not, could not bear the cost of absorbing a vast new population of exiles. Already blistered by criticism of his reversals on Haiti, Clinton needed a firm solution that would slow the flood of refugees but not ignore their suffering or antagonize the powerful Cuban-American community in Florida.

Clinton enjoyed a certain amount of maneuvering room: there is no significant sentiment in Congress to open up immigration or lift the trade embargo on Cuba. "The solution is not for 100,000 Cubans to come to the U.S.," says New Jersey Democrat Robert Menendez, "but for one man to leave Cuba, and that is Fidel Castro." While some angry Cuban Americans took to the streets of Miami shouting, "Down with Clinton!" exile leaders like

Jorge Mas Canosa, chairman of the powerful Cuban American National Foundation, lobbied the White House to keep up the pressure. The truth is that even the exiles don't want another Mariel, fearing a mass emigration would buy Castro more time. "I'm really struck by the reaction of the Cuban Americans," says one Senate staff member. "It appears that they don't want to give Castro a safety valve."

Some in Cuba, however, doubted the policy change would be any more of a deterrent than the sharks, the hunger, the stormy seas that refugees were already braving. In the Havana suburb of Miramar, the news that boat people would be detained did not deter a young Cuban who was hurrying to finish his raft. "I'll take my chances," he said. "They won't send us back."

Actually, that is just what the state of Florida would like to do. Already reeling from the moral and physical pressure of Haitians desperate to come to its shores, Florida called on Washington to admit that the situation had all the makings of a crisis. Governor Lawton Chiles declared an "immigration state of emergency," allowing him to call out the National Guard to help rescue, shelter and screen refugees. He demanded that Washington help defray the costs of health care, social services and law enforcement for the newcomers, which he estimates will approach $1 billion. . . . "All of us feel for rafters," Chiles said Saturday [Aug. 27, 1994], "but Florida cannot stand another influx."

They are young and old, peasants and professionals, pregnant women and children. They came in rafts made of ropes and inner tubes, catamarans built in living rooms, boats made from beds and old car engines. One young boy survived the journey after his parents gave him their only life jacket and handed him over to another boat—before they themselves disappeared beneath the waves. A group of rafters watched in horror as the limb of a fellow refugee floated by; he had gone crazy from hallucinations and had jumped into the ocean, only to be attacked by a shark.

A group of eleven floated up onto the fine white sands of Hallandale beach on the roof of a bus, which they had saved their money for years to buy. When they finally saw lights after eight days at sea, "we didn't know it was Miami, but we knew it couldn't be Havana," says Jorge Luis Díaz, 29, "because there's no electricity there, and no lights." As they gratefully reunited with family members in Little Havana, Attorney General Reno was announcing the new U.S. detention policy. Unaware of their close call, they all had one goal in mind. "To work!" they yelled in chorus.

The exodus follows nearly five years of increasing turmoil in Cuba after the fall of its Soviet patrons. Since 1989, imports have dropped from $8 billion to $2 billion. Last summer Castro eased a few restrictions. Possession of U.S. currency is no longer illegal, and some private employment is allowed. The timid reforms raised hopes for improved living standards. But a year later, with Castro blocking liberalization, and tensions erupting between the haves and the have-nots, refugees say hope has died. Ration books provide barely two weeks' worth of food. For the rest, families must rely on the black market, where 120 to 150 pesos, generally half a month's salary, buys only one U.S. dollar. "We had been waiting four or five months for soap. Everybody has got skin diseases, so we're taking baths with leaves now," says Elvis the bakery worker.

The pressure has grown all summer as gas, cigarette and food prices continued to climb. Residents of the capital began riding the ferry across Havana Bay four or five times a day, hoping it would be hijacked to Key West. Other Cubans began to commandeer motorboats and tugboats, but the authorities gave chase and opened fire. On July 13, [1994] at least thirty-two people died on the tugboat *Trece de Marzo* after it was rammed and sunk by pursuing Cuban ships. Aug. 5, [1994] saw the largest antigovernment demonstrations since Castro came to power.

Angered by the death of a policeman in a refugee hijacking in early August [1994], Castro threatened to open the ports and unleash the population. "Castro appeared on national television and said military police would no longer patrol the waterfront," explained Eugenia Ventacourt, 44, a former executive secretary from Havana. Like hundreds of others, she crept down to the coast to see whether police were still patrolling. Before dawn . . . she and ten others slipped away from a beach east of Havana. They were spotted by a Cuban coastal patrol boat 28 miles from the island, far beyond the coastal limits, but after circling their crudely built wooden craft, the soldiers let them proceed.

Those who did brave the sea seem to have come away from the ordeal with a better understanding of the price of freedom. "I don't want to wake up from my dream," exclaimed Aylen Alvarez, 8, a pretty girl from Puente Grande Havana who arrived . . . with her mother. "I want to eat the whole apple. I've never had one before. Can't I do that? Please?"

CUBA AND ITS EXILES[2]

Cuban affairs drew many headlines in 1994. Spring marked the beginning of a headlong cascade of events: a bungled attempt by the Havana regime to stage a dialogue with moderate exiles in April, a mass exodus of Cuban *balseros* (rafters) to U.S. shores in July and August, subsequent bilateral meetings with the United States throughout early fall, a November solidarity gathering in Cuba with what remains of the Latin American left, a non-invitation to Miami's Summit of the Americas in early December, the Vatican's appointment of a new Cuban cardinal in mid-December, an ongoing debate over the encampment of nearly thirty thousand Cubans in Guantanamo, rioting by Cubans in Panama, more bilateral meetings to discuss immigration and perhaps the economic blockade scheduled for early 1995, and so forth.

The list goes on, but the impasse remains. Still no opening in sight for bridging the thirty-six-year-old rift between Cuba and Washington. Or is it between Cuba and Miami? Cuba remains trapped in a series of historical binds: the lingering cult of a revolutionary leader turned omnipotent dictator, a controlled economy suddenly submitted to the law of neoliberal markets, the remnants of a cold war with the United States, and most important, a long-distance civil war with a transplanted ruling class in Miami still thirsting for revenge. Castro and Más Canosa (head of the Cuban-American Foundation) are both opposed to constructive negotiations among Cubans. One is now aiming to extract yet more sacrifices from three generations of self-denying revolutionaries facing economic collapse. The other seeks to fuel the pretense that there was no need for a revolution in the first place. Meanwhile, Cuba has become the only country left in the Western

[2]Article by Román de la Campa, professor of Latin American Studies and Comparative Literature at the State University of New York at StonyBrook, from *Dissent* 42:207–9 Spring '95. Copyright © 1995 by *Dissent*. Reprinted with permission.

hemisphere whose families are kept apart for strictly political reasons.

Most Americans believe the time has come to end the decades-long U.S. blockade on Cuba's economy. Even the *Wall Street Journal* and the late Richard Nixon dismissed its value. The growing consensus is that capitalism will undo the revolution sooner than any other measure. Besides, Americans are not accustomed to having restrictions placed on where they travel or invest, particularly after the collapse of the Soviet empire. Prolonging a feud with Castro also seems pointless after the demise of the socialist economy, unless one is bent on punishing Cubans who don't take to the seas. And if trading with China is acceptable, why not deal with Cuba? Does anyone really believe China has more respect for human rights than Cuba? A 1994 UN vote on the blockade left the United States practically alone against the world.

But such conventional wisdom fails to take into account the influential Cuban-American community—its stakes in the Cuba question, its importance in contemporary American politics, and its fears that Castro will retain or even strengthen his hold on power. One can't simply apply the cold, broad strokes of geopolitical calculation where there is an internal community capable of claiming a role in policy formation. Our Cuba policy is inextricably bound to the influence of Miami's Cuban community—a sort of exile nation within the United States built with the conviction that it holds a special position in contemporary American history. No other group of immigrants commands a measure like the "Cuban Adjustment Act of 1965," the U.S. law guaranteeing immediate residency and expedited citizenship to all Cubans who reach American territories.

Over the last thirty-six years, Miami has absorbed three distinct migration waves from Cuba. First came the "historical exile" of the early sixties, then the Mariel boatlift of 1980, and finally the recent exodus of "raft-people." But class, racial, and ideological differences have been masked by the wealth and power of the first group, some 200,000 upper-class and middle-class professionals, many of them first-generation Cubans of Spanish ancestry who were politically and economically displaced (and in some cases victimized) by the revolution. Upon arrival, they received immediate political asylum and considerable financial assistance from the U.S. government. Within a few decades, they transformed Miami from a provincial tourist town into a thriving Latin capital. Cuban immigrants from subsequent waves, such as those waiting in Guantanamo, have long known they can find immediate work and credit in this Spanish-speaking enclave of U.S. capitalism.

Consider the historical role played by the exile Cuban nation in U.S. politics. In the early sixties it galvanized America's fear of a spreading revolution led by Che, Fidel, Allende, Bishop, and ultimately Sandino. True enough, neither Kennedy nor subsequent presidents delivered the much-awaited successful invasion of Cuba on their behalf. But Cuban exiles were given a free hand to fashion Miami after their most cherished memories of pre-revolutionary Havana. By and large, Miami's Cubans and U.S. elites have created a community of mutual interests.

Now, however, all bets are off. Cubans in Guantanamo find themselves in a new era that features Proposition 187 and a U.S. commitment to legal immigration from Cuba. In this uncharted post-contra period of GATT and NAFTA, both Miami and Cuba must revise their scripts in response to shifting U.S. interests. Accordingly, Castro is moving toward the Chinese model of external market relations with internal political controls, while Más Canosa is threatening all foreign governments who dare invest in Cuba. In a recent letter to various embassies, he warns that a future Cuban government will place all the assets of those who deal with Castro in a trust until the losses incurred by the first wave of Cuban exiles are paid off.

Is there room for Cubans from both sides to step beyond this huge ideological divide? Not easily. Castro remains the only voice of power in Cuba. In Miami, there are more than fifty organized political groups, most of them with leaders from the Batista period of Cuban politics. All agree in their opposition to Castro but disagree on who should take power when he is finally overthrown. Each has its own candidate for president. But Más Canosa's Cuban-American Foundation is the only exile organization powerful enough to have a lobby in Washington and an agenda for the exile nation.

Nonetheless, it is clear that a growing number of working-class Cubans from the last migration wave favor a less drastic policy toward Cuba. They are more affected by measures against traveling and sending money to Cuba than exiles from earlier waves. Moreover, their memories of Cuba are fresher and perhaps more realistic; they are also likely to be less Americanized and have many more family members waiting for currency or a visa.

There have been two attempts to stage talks between the two Cubas—one in 1979, the other in 1994. Both were sponsored by Havana against Miami's opposition. In each instance Miami berated all participants and ridiculed the good will of independent exiles willing to talk. In Cuba these exiles also found their sentiments betrayed, as the sponsors exerted absolute control over the meetings. But perhaps the time has come for another try, this time under the auspices of a third party—say Mexico or Canada—with OAS (Organization of American States) supervision. A most likely convener for such a dialogue could be the new Cuban cardinal, Jaime Ortega. His credentials are impeccable: neither Cuba nor Miami trusts him completely. The immediate agenda is clear: allow Cuban families to see and help each other across the political divide without limitations, release the 30,000 Cubans from Guantanamo and Panama so they can enter the United States, review or repeal the Cuban Adjustment Act of 1965 so Cuba does not blame another exodus on it, promote and monitor legal mechanisms for emigration from Cuba. Needless to say, much larger and trickier questions lie beyond these small steps. But they could be the beginning of a bridge over a thirty-six-year-old breach.

THE NEW SLAVE TRADE[3]

Terrible as the past . . . had been, nothing could have prepared the 281 Chinese passengers on the freighter Golden Venture for their landfall in America. It was 2 a.m. and their ship, a dismal rust bucket never intended for human cargo, had just run aground off Rockaway Peninsula in New York. Pandemonium reigned on deck. Buffeted by six-foot ocean swells, the Golden Venture creaked and rolled as the frightened travelers peered toward the distant lights onshore. Then, urged on by shouting crewmen, scores of would-be immigrants abandoned their meager possessions and clambered down the vessel's sides for the dangerous, 200-yard swim to what they knew as *Meiguo,* "the beautiful country"—in this case, Queens.

[3]Article by Melinda Liu, *Newsweek* staff writer, from *Newsweek* 121:34–36, 41 Je 21 '93. Copyright © 1993 by Newsweek, Inc. All rights reserved. Reprinted with permission.

Six of them died in the attempt, while nearly 300 others, including the ship's captain and the twelve-man crew, were rounded up by New York City cops, U.S. immigration agents and the coast guard in one of the strangest rescue operations ever seen on American shores. As helicopters clattered overhead and coast guard launches circled the stranded freighter, hundreds of dazed and exhausted Chinese were pulled from the ship and the surrounding water and ferried to the beach. Most seemed grateful for the blankets, food and medical attention they got. Although a handful managed to elude authorities and vanish, survivors did not resist when they were led off to jail. "I was scared the Americans would push our boat back into the ocean," twenty-three-year-old Lin Jiantong said afterward. "If that happened, we were all going to jump."

In their hope and desperation—their absolute determination to come to America to build a better life—the Golden Venture's passengers are no different from the millions of European emigrants who passed through Ellis Island early in this century. But times have changed, and so has U.S. law. Lin and his fellow travelers have been detained as illegal aliens and may yet face deportation back to China. The ship's captain and ten crew members, along with one passenger, have been charged with alien-smuggling. (Court-appointed lawyers said the crew had no knowledge of the purpose of the voyage.) According to U.S. officials, all are only part of a much larger pattern of illegal immigration from Hong Kong, Taiwan and mainland China that now brings more than 100,000 undocumented Chinese to this country every year—and leaves many in virtual servitude.

This clandestine immigration is orchestrated by Chinese criminal syndicates operating in this country and Asia, federal officials say, and it is now a multibillion-dollar business. They say the smugglers, known as "snakeheads" to the Chinese, charge their clients anywhere from $20,000 to $50,000 apiece for transportation to America, and that every conceivable method is used to bring the illegals onto U.S. soil. Some come by plane, using forged documents, and some by foot, walking across the U.S. border from Mexico. Increasingly, these law-enforcement sources say, the Chinese gangs are turning to ships like the Golden Venture to deliver aliens all along the U.S. coastline. Since 1991, U.S. authorities have spotted forty vessels carrying thousands of Chinese aliens toward North America and intercepted twenty-four of them. But the ships keep coming. "We can't send our people, like

Barbary pirates, out to interdict vessels on the high seas," says Jack Shaw, head of investigations for the U.S. Immigration and Naturalization Service. "Meanwhile, they're coming from every direction, every ocean—the Pacific, the Atlantic, the Caribbean. There are too many oceans, too many ships."

The Golden Venture's 17,000-mile odyssey is a harrowing illustration of this illicit trade. Law-enforcement sources said the ship was won in a high-stakes card game by a young Chinese named Ah Kay, the reputed chieftain of the Fuk Ching gang in New York's Chinatown. These sources said the ship acquired a Burmese captain and a mixed-nationality crew in Hong Kong in January. It then sailed into the South China Sea for a rendezvous off Bangkok with small craft carrying about ninety paying passengers—who happily shouted "America! America!" as the voyage began. After a stop in Singapore, the Golden Venture headed for Mombasa, Kenya, where about 200 more Chinese came on board. These would-be immigrants, left stranded in Mombasa by another smuggling ship, crowded into the Golden Venture's darkened hold for what would soon become the most terrifying experience of their lives.

So bitter: The Golden Venture left Mombasa and headed south, toward the Cape of Good Hope and the long passage across the Atlantic to the East Coast of the United States. Somewhere near the cape, the ship encountered a ferocious storm that left both passengers and crew in fear for their lives. The ship survived, but conditions on board got steadily worse. Each passenger was allotted barely enough room to lie down. There were no showers, and there was only one toilet for 281 people. "We brushed our teeth with salt water. We got skin rashes from washing with water from the sea," one passenger said. "Twenty days, that's how long they said the voyage would be. But it was long, so bitter, so hard. They never said it would be so bitter." Food—rice and vegetables, cooked on hot plates in the hold—was scarce, and the passengers fought among themselves to see who would get the most. "A lot of fighting was going on," a survivor told a reporter. "I think it changed many people, being on that ship."

And it got worse. U.S. officials said some of the twenty-seven women aboard had been sexually abused during the voyage, though they did not say by whom. They also said a passenger, identified in court records as Kin Sin Lee, staged a mutiny as the Golden Venture neared the U.S. coast. Other passengers described Lee as a "trustee" or enforcer for smugglers who organized the voyage. "He was just like us in the beginning, just a normal guy like me," one passenger said. "But gradually over the three months, he became like a leader." The mutiny probably occurred because the ship twice failed to keep a planned rendezvous with U.S.-based fishing boats that were to carry the passengers ashore—probably to the Boston area, according to investigators.

At the weekend, all but four of the passengers were still behind bars. INS officials said their detention reflected the Clinton administration's determination to deter the continuing influx of Chinese illegal aliens—but if so, Washington may be forced to revise its current policies toward Chinese immigration. According to some Chinese-American community leaders, both the smugglers and their clients are well aware that Chinese illegals can avoid deportation by claiming political asylum under U.S. law. These critics point to changes in federal policy during the Reagan and Bush administrations that had the effect of making it easier for Chinese nationals to claim asylum. Though the primary goal of these policies was to protect Chinese dissidents from deportation, the net effect was to clog the INS appeals system with thousands of asylum petitions. In most cases, the INS is required to release illegal aliens who file asylum claims, and that has allowed many illegals to melt into Chinese communities in cities like New York.

They may be better off in jail. According to New York City police investigators, Chinese illegal aliens face ruthless exploitation by the same gangs that brought them to America. Few of the illegals are able to pay the smugglers' fee in advance. That means they arrive in cities like New York owing huge sums to the smugglers, who send enforcers to collect installment payments on the debt. As a result, many are forced to work eighteen-hour days at menial jobs for substandard wages, always with the threat of deportation over their heads—and others are forced into prostitution, gambling and crime. "It's like involuntary servitude to organized-crime groups," says the FBI's Jim Moody. "Some, not all, stay with crime for the rest of their lives." Those who fail to pay the gangs face kidnapping, torture and death. . . . New York police raided a "safe house" in Brooklyn and freed thirteen Chinese illegals allegedly being held by the Fuk Ching gang.

Lt. Joseph Pollini, head of the NYPD's major-case squad, says Fuk Ching is now the most powerful gang in Chinatown. Its reputed leader, twenty-eight-year-old Ah Kay, is believed by New

York police and federal authorities to be the mastermind behind the Golden Venture's voyage. Police say that Ah Kay, also known as Guo Liang Chi, was convicted of attempted grand larceny and served two years in prison before being deported to China in 1988. He returned to the United States in 1989, was arrested and convicted of criminal re-entry. In 1991 he, too, filed a claim for political asylum, effectively blocking deportation. Meanwhile, according to police, Ah Kay consolidated his grip on the Fuk Ching gang and its alien-smuggling operations. Late last year, police sources say, Ah Kay and another Fuk Ching member got into a dispute, probably over money. Their feud may have led to a shoot-out in Chinatown last January and to a gang-style hit last month in suburban Teaneck, N.J. According to police there, a group of armed Asian men invaded a home and killed four young Chinese, including two of Ah Kay's brothers.

Heroin trade: The rise of Chinese organized crime and Chinese alien-smuggling have federal law-enforcement officials worried. Both have their roots in the gradual relaxation of the Beijing government's control over southern China—particularly Fujian province, where corrupt government officials have reportedly helped the smugglers load ships just like the Golden Venture. The Fujianese are also increasingly active in the international heroin trade. Since February, Fujianese criminals have been involved in six out of eight major heroin busts by the U.S. Drug Enforcement Administration's Group 41, a New York-based unit that specializes in Southeast Asian drug traffickers. "Except for the fact that they're Chinese, the suspects looked just like Italian wiseguys," a DEA source says. And that's the real goal for knowledgeable law-enforcement officials—preventing Chinese gangs from becoming a deep-rooted problem like the Cosa Nostra.

So the Golden Venture's passengers are pawns in a much larger game—a struggle to protect Chinese immigrants from being victimized by their own countrymen, a diplomatic controversy between Washington and Beijing, and the never-ending war against drugs. Critics of the INS, like Arthur Helton, director of the Refugee Project of the Lawyer's Committee for Human Rights, say the Feds are wrong to make an example of the survivors by keeping them in jail. But veteran cops like Raymond Kelly, New York's commissioner of police, are convinced that their release, if it comes, will only lead to the "tragedy" of further oppression by the mob. But how long can they be held and what happens next? Like any policy abstraction, this one ultimately has a human face. "We risked our lives to come here," said a twenty-three-year-old Golden Venture survivor named Zhang Hairong. "I'd rather die than go back—but then, I feel like I've died many times already."

CHINA'S HUMAN TRAFFICKERS[4]

Mr. Zheng from Wenzhou, China, may be unlucky to have been one of the passengers on the ill-fated Golden Venture, which rammed the shore of Queens more than a year ago. He is, however, the envy of his fellow inmates at the Metropolitan Detention Center in lower Manhattan, because his wife comes to see him *every day* during visiting hours. Theirs is a story of bitter irony. Mrs. Zheng, who came to America illegally three years ago, understood right away that it was not what it was cracked up to be, considering the harsh working conditions, low wages and unbearable pressure of paying off a $30,000 debt to her "snakehead" (human smuggler) within three years. She advised her husband to hold off on his plans to come. Unfortunately, Zheng took that to mean that she had found someone else, so he decided to leave their four-year-old daughter with his parents and started his own journey to the States—first by bus to the China-Burma border, then on foot through the jungle to Thailand. Mrs. Zheng found this out only when he cabled from Bangkok asking for $1,700 to pay for the cost of continuing the journey. The snakehead had promised passage by plane to New York; Zheng ended up boarding a ship that took him to Singapore, then to Mauritius in the Indian Ocean and finally to Kenya. There, he waited for six months before embarking on the Golden Venture with nearly 300 other Chinese immigrants. The rest is history.

Mrs. Zheng, an ever-devoted wife, has retained a lawyer, and has been assiduously lobbying human rights and church groups to fight for her husband's release. It has not been easy. She does not speak English and works eleven hours a day as a seamstress in a Chinese-owned garment factory on Seventh Avenue, then trav-

[4]Article by Peter Kwong, director of the Asian American Studies Program at Hunter College, from *The Nation* 259:422–25 O 19 '94. Copyright © 1994 by The Nation Company, L.P. Reprinted with permission.

els back to her Queens apartment, which she shares with five other "snake people," undocumented workers from Wenzhou. After dinner, she spends two more hours at her sewing machine assembling pieces she has taken home from the factory. With all the unanticipated expenses involving her husband, she has yet to pay off half her own "transportation fee," as she puts it. Somewhat bitterly, she asks: "Hundreds of illegals are still coming from China every week. So why is my husband still in jail? We are, after all, law-abiding and decent people." She urged me and two other American journalists to visit Wenzhou and see for ourselves.

The Zheng family lives on the rural outskirts of Wenzhou, which is in Zhejiang Province, more than 200 miles south of Shanghai. Its inhabitants are known for their seafaring heritage as well as their entrepreneurship. In recent years, fueled by investments from the overseas Chinese in Taiwan and Hong Kong, Wenzhou has become part of the booming economy of southern China that has captured so much attention abroad. Wenzhou claims to be the button-manufacturing center of the world. It is also the second-largest source of illegal emigration from China after Fuzhou, which lies to its south.

Once in Wenzhou, we took a ferry, a bus and a pedicab to get to the Zhengs'. After viewing the videotape we had shot of Mr. Zheng in his yellow prison garb, his mother wept. "He has aged so much—all skin and bones. I can't believe that's him. We always thought America was a humane country. How can you lock him up like this for so long like an animal?"

We explained to the grieving family that the Clinton Administration is caught in a public relations dilemma. It cannot release the Golden Venture inmates lest it encourage more illegals, invoking the specter of the "yellow peril" from antiimmigrant groups. Conversely, it faces reproach from humanitarian groups and those critical of the Chinese government's record on human rights, including conservative right-to-life organizations who denounce China's "one child" policy (the basis for the inmates' plea for political asylum). We suggested that their son might soon be released, or at least returned to China, after public attention drifts away from the issue.

Mother Zheng leapt up in alarm at the last suggestion: "No! No! They cannot send him back! That would be the death of this family. I'll commit suicide." Her daughter revealed that they had already borrowed money at a high interest rate for Zheng's journey, expecting to be paid back as soon as he started working in

America. Now that he is in prison, they have to keep borrowing just to pay off the interest. If he were sent back to China, the family would have no way of coming up with that large a sum, not to mention the fines and imprisonment the Chinese authorities might impose on him.

The Zhengs are not the only family in this dire predicament. As news of our presence spread, other families who had relatives on the Golden Venture began to appear. Of the 276 Golden Venture inmates, forty are from the Wenzhou area (the rest are from Fuzhou) and twenty-five are from Zheng's village and neighboring Jiudu Island. Surprisingly, almost all of the few thousand residents of the region are Christians. We were told that the local congregation had a sixty-year history, predating the Communist revolution. On our first evening there, a Sunday, the minister invited us to attend a special prayer service for the Golden Venture prisoners. Of the 300 who attended, seventy-five were relatives; the congregation's sobs and anguished prayers made it clear that this community has suffered a major calamity.

They have no contact with American authorities, and the Chinese government has maintained strict silence on the matter. Sixty-six-year-old Mrs. Peng, whose only daughter is languishing in a Louisiana prison, mourned, "We are totally in the dark." The villagers looked to us for help, and the minister in his prayer compared us to "angels from heaven" who were sent to spread the word to the American public that his are honest people deserving freedom.

Mr. Sung, once a small-time Communist Party cadre, has four family members imprisoned in the United States, including his daughter. "We are simply trying to make a better life for ourselves by going to America." He explained that while Deng Xiaoping's market reforms had initially improved conditions in the countryside—as evidenced by the number of small-scale factories dotting the rural landscape—the benefits have not lasted. After an increasing number of people began making shoes and clothing, profit margins declined and markets dried up. "We are left to fend for ourselves in highly risky businesses. Without government connections, we can't export our goods. Where can we sell our products?" As it is, Sung's son is desperately attempting to make contacts in Manchuria in order to get rid of a warehouse full of men's dress shoes. There are thriving black markets near the Russian border. But to get anything done in China these days, people have to bribe officials with gifts and banquets just to procure a license. "Without name-brand cigarettes or a twelve-course banquet, they wouldn't lift a finger."

In view of this situation, Sung and the elders in the family raised thousands of dollars to pay the snakeheads to smuggle the young to America. "We thought it would be easier to make money in the United States. Once they make enough to send home, the elders can retire from the fields and the family can build houses and pay for daughters' weddings, and as members of an 'overseas family,' we also gain respectability."

These family plans have turned into nightmares. Zheng's parents still live in the oldest and smallest house on their block. The Sungs had to rent part of their compound to a local factory, and the head of the household, a great-grandfather who is nearly eighty, had to harvest and thresh rice under the brutal July sun. Mrs. Peng, whose imprisoned daughter was the family's only source of income, now has to do all the heavy field work and feed the pigs.

The reality is that privatization in China has brought opportunities and unchecked competition, but only those who are young, ambitious and ruthless can prosper. And even these few need political connections, since Communist officials have monopolized the most lucrative enterprises. Members of the party are the first to benefit from the transition to capitalism.

China is polarized in more ways than one. The country's development is predicated on an export-oriented economy financed by foreign investment, so growth is concentrated in the southern coastal areas near Hong Kong and Taiwan. With decollectivization, all transactions must be in cash. People from the interior and remote rural areas without such development are now migrating south and inundating cities like Wenzhou and Fuzhou, where they wait at street corners, bus stops and train stations, hoping to be hired as day laborers. According to the Chinese government's own statistics, some fifty million people are roaming the country looking for jobs. Among this floating population are begging street urchins, barefoot and dressed in rags. Scabby-headed, flies gathering in the corners of their eyes, their presence recalls the severe deprivation of pre-1949 China.

Labor organizing is prohibited. In fact, labor leaders were the first to be rounded up after the June 4, 1989, Tiananmen Square massacre. In the unregulated labor market, factory owners, including foreign companies, prefer out-of-province workers because they are "less demanding and work harder." The highly

profitable Reebok shoe factory in the city of Fuzhou, located in a
huge complex in the vicinity of the city's free-enterprise zone,
attracts few city workers precisely because of its low wages and
long hours.

This rural-to-urban, north-to-south migration has brought
inflation, congestion, depressed wages, high unemployment and
social disorder to cities in the infant stages of industrial development. Chinese reforms have created a chain reaction of massive
human displacement with international consequences. And it's
not just people at the bottom of the social scale who want to leave
the country. The families of Golden Venture inmates are not
badly off by Chinese standards, or else they have relatives abroad.
Otherwise, they could not possibly have come up with the $1,500
down payment for the illegal trips. Others borrow from the community's rotating credit systems.

We met a young taxi driver who had flown into Japan three
times on a phony passport provided by the snakeheads at an
enormous cost. She was turned back at the Narita airport each
time. Then she tried to smuggle herself into the United States in a
sealed container under the deck of a cargo ship, but was discovered after four days at sea and repatriated. Undaunted, she is
trying again: "If you want to make something of yourself, even if
it is to find a good husband, you have to get out." Thousands of
disillusioned Chinese, like her, desperately want to leave the
country.

People like the taxi driver are ready victims for snakeheads.
Fuzhou, a city similar to but even more dynamic than Wenzhou, is
known to be the capital of snakeheads. In this multibillion-dollar
international operation, lower-ranking smugglers roam the city
competing for customers. Pretending that we wanted to help a
friend get to the States, we had no trouble finding them. In fact,
just hanging around a cafe and a candy store, we met four in one
afternoon. Their average fee is $33,000, with $1,500 down and
the rest to be paid upon arrival in New York (usually by relatives
already in the United States who are then paid back within three
years at a 3 percent interest rate). Each smuggler promised a
better deal: U.S. entry by plane, a money-back guarantee in case
of failure, a fifty-fifty split with the customer for the cost of bail
and lawyer's fee if caught.

The Chinese government hardly interferes; it has long considered overseas Chinese a national asset. As more and more
people leave, unemployment decreases and foreign-exchange re-

mittances flow in from abroad. Government departments are known to have organized "official" cultural, trade and business delegations to foreign countries so that employees and their relatives could leave the country permanently. We even came across a government agency in charge of exporting technical personnel. Its deputies are known to have sold to ordinary citizens at black-market prices work visas, issued by foreign governments. Having reached their destination, these so-called experts disappear, remaining under the control of "enforcers," who make sure they honor the "transportation fee." In these cases the government acts—and profits—as the snakehead.

Chinese human smuggling entails an elaborate and sophisticated international network, which is said to be financed and masterminded in Taiwan. The whole operation is like a global baseball game. Most often, the sprint to first base involves the transfer of would-be immigrants from Fuzhou or Wenzhou to international waters, where they are picked up by Taiwanese cargo ships or fishing boats. After each vessel is fully loaded (the shipping companies are paid by the head), it sails south to Thailand for refueling before making the dash to second base, across the Pacific to the coast of Central America or Mexico. The southern sea route is specifically chosen to avoid detection by U.S. reconnaissance satellites monitoring American coastal waters. (The path selected by the Golden Venture—making a landing off the American shoreline—is the most risky and least popular route.) Having landed, the smuggling crew escorts its charges to third base, crossing the U.S. border by land. If the ship comes ashore in Central America, the immigrants travel through Mexico City, cross the border clandestinely and arrive in Houston. If they land in the Baja peninsula of Mexico, they cross into San Diego and rest in safe houses in Monterey Park before making their way to New York.

The most comfortable route is, of course, by plane. The trick is to fly to an airport where ground security is so lax, or more likely so corrupt, that it allows Chinese with questionable identification papers to board planes heading for the United States. This may mean traveling via Budapest or Moscow. Once in the United States they either pass through immigration controls undetected or, if detected, request political asylum. The air route is much chancier than the sea route and considerably less profitable for the snakeheads.

The success of human smuggling operations depends on the

cooperation of hundreds of individuals, including corrupt officials in China, fishermen-smugglers on China's coast, Taiwanese freight owners, Malaysian shipping crews, operators of safe houses dotting the globe, corrupt immigration officials and underworld connections all along the route from Bangkok, Central America, Mexico and Texas to New York.

The United States is not the only destination the snakeheads offer; Australia, the Netherlands and Argentina are also popular. But Japan is the favorite—there one can save more than $2,000 a month, and on a strictly enforced eight-hour workday. Passage to the United States is the most expensive, even though the illegals make less under unregulated labor conditions. Once here, because of lax enforcement, they can work without fear of the harassment, arrests or deportations that are regular occurrences in Japan and France.

Zheng's lawyer contends that the only reason the Golden Venture people were imprisoned is that they came in such large numbers and in such a dramatic way. The Immigration and Naturalization Service, embarrassed, had to act tough to maintain its image. In fact, anyone arriving in the United States can request political asylum. He or she is then usually released and becomes eligible for a temporary work permit. Then immigration officials require the individual to appear at a court hearing.

The I.N.S.'s effectiveness should be seen in the context of America's demand for cheap labor. For some time now the U.S. economy has been emphasizing growth through deregulation and increased labor productivity. The most effective way to achieve this is by employing nonunionized labor. Immigrant labor is even better, because it is not organized and even less protected. Following this logic, undocumented labor is the best: entirely unregulated and thus the most productive. In the case of Chinese from Fuzhou and Wenzhou, they are not only undocumented but are indentured and are willing to work under almost any conditions to avoid punishment or harm to their families in China.

So many illegals have been coming that relatives in the States are burdened with debts they cannot pay. In that case, the new arrivals are forced to borrow from the snakeheads themselves—at 30 percent interest. These undocumented immigrants, with no knowledge of English, can only get jobs that earn less than $1,000 a month, not even enough to pay interest on the loan. The snakeheads hire enforcers to beat up debtors who evade their obligations. A favorite tactic is to threaten the victim's relatives with his imminent execution so they will come up with some quick cash.

In some cases, the snakeheads simply make the debtors their virtual slaves. During the day, the victims work at restaurants that have been linked to organized crime. At night, after they are brought back to prisonlike dorms, they hand over all their money and are locked up until the next day.

Sadly, there is no shortage of employers, Chinese and non-Chinese, looking for their services. The demand for these "unfree" laborers and organized labor's lack of interest in defending them as part of the American working class help expand the Chinese human smuggling operation, the Golden Venture publicity notwithstanding. Snakeheads are recruiting more and more innocents to be enslaved. Their greed is now the driving force of Chinese immigration. They have even devised a propaganda and misinformation campaign to lure new prospects.

When we confronted our friends in China with the abuses perpetrated by the snakeheads, the response was that some illegals deserved to be punished because they were lazy and unwilling to work hard to pay off their debts. In the meantime, Zheng's younger sister blames her brother's troubles on the blundering of his snakehead. She is going to America as soon as she can find a "good" one.

When we mentioned the hardship of the illegals, one older farmer stared me in the eye and said: "Look, I work on fourmou land [less than one acre, larger than average holding] year in and year out, from dawn to dusk, but after taxes and providing for our own needs, I make $20 a year. You make that much in a day. No matter how much it costs to get there, or how hard the work is, America is still better than this."

THE OVERACHIEVERS[5]

The wormy underside of the gorgeous mosaic is on open view in Brooklyn Criminal Court, Part AP-9, Judge Karen Yellen presiding. Petty thieves, drunk drivers, and wife beaters, immigrants from a hundred different countries, come to this flea market of justice to negotiate their fates. Judgment is rendered in the time

[5]Article by Jeffrey Goldberg, contributing editor of *New York*, from *New York* 28:42–51 Ap 10 '95. Copyright © 1995 by Jeffrey Goldberg. Reprinted with permission of International Creative Management, Inc.

it takes to boil water, and many of the lawyers don't even know the judge's name. "It's like with the Sicilians," one lawyer whispers. "You try not to remember the name of the person you despise."

Judge Yellen is no easy mark, certainly, and on this particular morning, Henry Jung, an assistant district attorney, is about to understand that. Jung is asking Judge Yellen to issue an order of protection to keep a defendant from harassing a woman; the judge evidently believes Jung is straying from the point. "You have to give a reason for an order of protection, Mr. Jung," she snaps.

"Our policy is—"

"Your policy does not impress me, Mr. Jung."

"This case involves a man standing before a woman displaying a broken bottle—"

"There is no reason to believe that these people will ever come into contact again," the judge says, shutting down the discussion.

Jung moves to his seat, shoulders hunched, and shakes off the defeat. A crackhead's snoring echoes through the courtroom.

As a child in South Korea, Henry Jung dreamed of an America that straddled the world like a great tiger. Brooklyn Criminal Court has bled the thirty-four-year-old of some of his idealism, but he knows, fifteen years after he moved to America, that he lives in a remarkable place. What other country would have let a twenty-year-old immigrant who spoke little English on arrival become a government prosecutor? There's no glory in Brooklyn Criminal Court, but it's a respectable first stop for an ambitious lawyer.

Several miles southeast of Judge Yellen's courtroom, on a tired side street in Sheepshead Bay, Hyo-Soon Jung, Henry's mother, stands behind the register of her failing grocery store, waiting for the rare customer. The old Jews who bought borscht and herring here have died; the Russian immigrants who repopulated the neighborhood in recent years do their shopping in Brighton Beach. The government, too, has hurt business—after Mrs. Jung let an old man buy a bar of soap and a can of beer with food stamps, the USDA kicked the Jungs off the program. Mrs. Jung is soft on old people who try to buy beer and soap with food stamps, but this old man was an undercover government operative. "I don't want the government's money anyway," she says. "That's why I have children."

Faded signs taped to the windows advertise soaps and snacks the store no longer carries. The Jungs' store is a poor cousin to the high-volume, 24-hour Korean-run groceries ubiquitous in Manhattan. Yet there's no dust on the shelves—that would be an embarrassment. And when a customer does happen by, Mrs. Jung musters a gentle smile and some soft words. But mostly she waits.

Business at the Korean markets throughout the city has slowed, but it's even slower here. Two years ago her husband died, and Mrs. Jung is running the store with the help of her younger son, Chang-keun. Henry helps on weekends, but it's still a burden, and Mrs. Jung doesn't seem to mind her recent decision to run her stock down and close up for good. She sits on a milk crate outside the still-open store, and while she professes to agonize about everything—"I never stop worrying"—her manner suggests a good deal of confidence in the future. "I always wanted Henry to be a lawyer," she says, taking in the sun, "and now he is one."

It's an odd and poignant victory. Mrs. Jung is a music teacher by training, and she took a giant step away from white-collar success when she came to America to sell and stack and sweep and count. Soon, she won't even have *that*. But her son Henry is a lawyer.

There are thousands of Koreans in New York like Hyo-Soon Jung, bright, cultured people who have sacrificed dreams of professional glory to ensure their children's success. A complex combination of factors persuaded Koreans to emigrate—the rigidity of Korean society, terrible overcrowding on the Korean peninsula. But when Koreans are asked why they came here, almost to a person they say it was to give their children a chance to learn in the best universities in the world. This is why Koreans may be remembered as the most instantly successful immigrant group in American history.

An old joke asks: What's the difference between the International Ladies' Garment Workers' Union and the American Psychiatric Association? The answer: One generation.

The joke is a comment on the quick march of immigrant Jews to professional glory, and it applies with equal relevance to the Koreans, because no group has replicated the Jewish formula for business and educational success with such efficiency.

In just three decades—before 1965, the year large-scale Asian immigration began, there were no more than 500 Koreans in the entire metropolitan area—the Koreans have changed the face of commercial New York, opening thousands of stores, rescuing whole neighborhoods from decay, and inventing entirely new retail industries in the process. In the New York region, Koreans own 1,400 produce stores (85 percent of all such stores in the area), 3,500 groceries, 2,000 dry cleaners, 800 seafood stores, and 1,300 nail salons, according to one Korean business group. "They are New York City's most productive community," Emanuel Tobier, a professor of economics at New York University, says unequivocally.

At the same time, the Koreans, who even now number no more than a quarter-million in the entire region, have reinvigorated dying neighborhoods and the schools—and churches—that anchor them. Today, high schools such as Cardozo and Bayside in Queens serve as petri dishes for Korean success, the role Erasmus and Midwood played in the golden age of Jewish academic achievement.

Historically and religiously, of course, Jews and Koreans have no common experience, but in twentieth-century America they overlap in an extraordinary number of ways. Both groups produce excellent violinists; poor black shoppers frequently despise them; in different ways, both feel marginalized by mainstream society; and Harvard Yard runs thick with them. Korean-Americans have even taken over deserted Jewish camps in the Catskills. They're used for church retreats.

The Jews hacked the widest path for immigrants culturally predisposed to mercantilism and educational overachievement, and it is because of this that many Korean-Americans have an almost psychological dependence on the Jewish experience. Some Korean-Americans even refer to themselves jokingly as "Kews."

There is a conscious choice here, one that reveals much about the changing dynamics of the melting pot. The Korean Students Association at Columbia University, for example, is the only minority group unwilling to participate in an umbrella body known, so awfully correctly, as the United Students of Color Council. The president of the Korean group, John Min, a pre-medical student from Washington State, explains why: "I'm not sure what agenda we have in common. My skin color"—he proffers his hand for inspection—"is closer to a Jewish shade than an Indian or black shade."

"We know that the Jews have been there before," says Grace Lyu-Volckhausen, a community activist and an unofficial ambassador of the Korean community to the outside world. "There's similar values, similar behaviors, similar experiences in America. There's a sense of determination in the Jewish community we can understand."

But Korean history in New York reads like an abridged version of the Jewish; Koreans are skipping whole chapters as they suburbanize and assimilate. They were never stuck in airless ghettos like the Lower East Side, and unlike Jews in the great waves of immigration eighty and ninety years ago, the Koreans were pulled here more than they were pushed. They arrived with college degrees—60 percent, by some estimates, have come with at least B.A.'s—and they've always been viewed as a "model minority" by the white majority.

This year marks the thirtieth anniversary of the passage of the act that allowed full-scale Asian immigration, and it should be an occasion for the Korean community to mark its obvious successes. But instead of celebrating, Korean New York is dogged by anxiety.

It is not racial strife that causes worry, though race is the prism through which the outside world most often sees the Korean community. The 1990 boycott was certainly frightening—many store owners feared that the picketing of a Flatbush grocery by blacks would inevitably mean a citywide boycott and violence, which it didn't. The Los Angeles riots felt more threatening, but they were experienced vicariously in New York.

The hair-pulling problem of the moment is economic, growing from the belief that New York's retail economy, struggling for breath since 1990, will never be robust again, and that City Hall, so concerned about seducing neighborhood-busting megastores to open here, is unaware that hundreds of Korean-owned stores, like the grocery owned by Hyo-Soon Jung in Brooklyn, are forced to shut each year.

"We're in the middle of a tragedy," says Sung Soo Kim, president of the Korean-American Small Business Service Center in Flushing, the capital of Korean New York. "Last year, we had 700 stores open but 900 close. Growth has completely stopped. We're having 15 percent turnover every year. People are closing up." Times are so tough, some Korean businessmen say, that one of the linchpins of Korean success in New York, the *keh*, or revolving-credit system, is itself in a state of slow collapse. (The *keh* relies on regular contributions from a group of friends to a communal pot. One of them receives the full amount each month, which he can use as seed capital.) "In 1986, 57 percent of the people were in *kehs*," Kim says. "But cash registers aren't growing now. People can't afford to give."

These setbacks are quickly percolating through the Korean community. "I just saw in Flushing 300 or 400 older Koreans lining up to get government cheese and butter at a senior center," says Jonathan Kim of the Asian-American Federation, a nonprofit advocacy group.

Long before Dan Quayle posited his thoughts on family values, Confucius had formulated his, and his teachings—which permeate all layers of Korean life—hold duty to family as a paramount virtue. Honorable men support their families; dishonorable ones don't. But, Jonathan Kim says, "it comes to a point where you forget about honor and you just go collect your cheese."

This sudden vulnerability is causing some first-generation Koreans to register a more fundamental anxiety: Why are they here at all? Many Koreans say that they feel essentially powerless: powerless in their own homes, as they watch America turn their children into people they don't fully understand—that is, Americans; powerless outside their homes, in the unnavigable world of coalition politics; and powerless in their own businesses, where they find they don't control the largest levers of economic success.

The Koreans seem to dominate whole sectors of New York's economy. But this apparent hegemony is deceptive, because they often have little control over the means of distribution or the buildings they sell from. At the Hunts Point market in the Bronx, where many Koreans go to buy produce, the overwhelming majority of wholesalers are Italian-American or Jewish. Even in the garment center, where 300 Korean-owned sweatshops employ thousands of Latino laborers, the notion of Korean power is chimeric. The sweatshops owned by Koreans, mixed in with shops owned by Chinese and other immigrant groups, are actually small contracting outfits that do the bidding of the big Seventh Avenue manufacturers, who in turn work for the designers and department stores.

In a gray building on Eighth Avenue near 37th Street, one of more than sixty nameless buildings that house, all told, 3,000 individual sweatshops, the Korean owner of one such shop talks about the choice he made to enter the garment industry. He asks that he be identified only by the name Kim, which is shared by a quarter of all Koreans. "I was educated at Yonsei University in South Korea," he says. Yonsei is the equivalent of Princeton. Only two schools, Seoul National (the Harvard) and Korea University (the Yale), are similarly prestigious.

Around Kim sit fifteen or so Hispanic women, sewing madly. Many of them, he admits, are undocumented aliens. The windows are blackened over, and lack of ventilation gives the room a damp, tight feel. Kim admits that his workers take home as little as $3 an hour and shakes his head ruefully when he says how much he takes home a week—$300. "Owning is not very profitable."

The small contractors are apparently so pitiable that they've even gained the sympathy of labor organizers. "A lot of times, the workers aren't getting paid by the contractors, but that's because the contractor isn't getting paid by the manufacturer," says Francisco Chang, a Korean-born ILGWU organizer.

"The manufacturer's tactic is to put the contractor against the wall and twist his arm. Many of these manufacturers will have auctions where they'll hold up a blouse and say, 'Five dollars.' The contractors will bid against each other, driving the price down. . . . The contractors see the manufacturers and the building owners, the Jews, as very powerful," Chang says. "They perceive that it is not worth the fight."

This is the flipside of the Korean-Jewish relationship, seldom if ever talked about. Officially, Korean-Jewish relations are grand—it is Jewish organizations, especially the Jewish Community Relations Council, that are helping the Korean community organize politically, and Jews and Koreans find comfort in each other's troubles with African-Americans.

But, says Professor Pyong Gap Min, a Korean-born sociologist at Queens College, many Koreans have ambivalent feelings about the Jews. They try to take the Jews as a model. On the other hand, they see the Jews as very stingy."

This sub rosa antipathy extends to the grocery stores, where a common bit of Korean folk wisdom held that opening a store in a Jewish neighborhood is a losing proposition, because Jews are cheap. Hyo-Soon Jung, Henry's mother, remembers hearing this when she and her late husband looked to open a store in Sheepshead Bay.

"There was a prejudice against opening up in a Jewish neighborhood, because the Jewish reputation is stingy," she says, perched on her milk crate. "This is not true. It is actually Jewish people who are the biggest spenders, as long as there is quality. As long as we sold high-quality fruit, the Jews came."

Not anymore, though. Mrs. Jung looks down East 17th Street, toward Kings Highway. "There's a Pathmark down there. That's where the Jewish ladies go to shop now. They're smart."

Everyone knows a Korean, and nobody knows a Korean. It's a weird conundrum of New York life. Here's a group that in less than thirty years has transformed New York's commercial culture and, with other Asians—most notably the Chinese—is saving the city's educational institutions from mediocrity and worse.

Yet it's impossible to name a famous Korean in New York. There are no Korean judges or police chiefs, no City Council members or assemblymen. Economically struggling, the Koreans are politically stunted. They raise money for non-Korean politicians—Rudy Giuliani was a favorite—but they have few effective lobbyists and no plausible candidates for public office.

A new, much-anticipated novel by a twenty-nine-year-old Korean-American writer named Chang-rae Lee tells the story of a Korean-born member of the New York City Council, a mayoral candidate who is worshiped by his multiethnic Queens constituency. *Native Speaker*—the first novel by a Korean-American to be brought out by a major publisher—is an artful meditation on ethnic identity, fractured loyalties, and cultural confusion that is bundled inside a not-entirely-plausible political spy thriller. Perhaps the most improbable aspect of *Native Speaker* is the very idea of a Korean-American running for mayor of New York. In 1995, this is sheer fantasy.

"What happens is that the narrator is so amazed that a Korean man of his generation could imagine a public identity for himself," Lee explains.

It is not that Korean immigrants don't want to join public society. If they felt they had to run for office to survive they would; the decision to build a citywide monopoly on 24-hour groceries was itself a rational response to their marginal status as just-off-the-plane immigrants. (It is a common stereotype that Korean culture is essentially mercantile, but in fact, their cultural traditions afford little special status to the businessman—"If one is guided by profit in one's actions, one will incur much ill will," Confucius wrote in *The Analects*.) As New York's Korean community becomes savvier about American life, it may find that there is much to gain in following the African-American model of exerting influence through electoral politics. In California, which has a much larger Korean community, Jay Kim, a San Bernardino Republican, in 1992 became the first Korean-American to be elected to Congress. And the upcoming Republican presidential primary will undoubtedly lead to a minor media frenzy on the issue of Koreans: Wendy Gramm, Phil Gramm's wife and an economist, is a third-generation Korean-American from Hawaii. She is about to become the most famous Korean in America.

Even if he weren't married to a Korean-American, Phil Gramm would provoke strong interest among first-generation Korean immigrants—his small-government, deregulation message speaks to a community that carved out its economic niche wholly outside the realm of officialdom. For many Koreans in business—and three fourths of Koreans in New York City do derive their livelihoods from small business, according to Sung Soo Kim, the Flushing business leader—government, with its OSHA inspectors and sanitation police and tax collectors, serves no salutary function.

Even with the husband of a Korean-American in the race, however, it's unlikely that older immigrants will choose en masse to retrofit their public profiles. "Many Koreans don't unpack their suitcases when they get here, so they don't have confidence in their ability to become Americans," says Grace Lyu-Volckhausen, the activist.

Lyu-Volckhausen has unpacked *her* suitcases, but she is an unusual case. Though she is a member of the pilgrim generation of Koreans in New York—she arrived to study in 1960, when there were fewer than 200 Koreans here—she stands outside the circle of first-generation leaders. She is a woman, for one thing, and she is married to a white man.

This puts her more in sync with the children of the immigrants, many of whom see their parents' generation as atomized and leaderless. Some younger Koreans say half kiddingly that they wish they had an Al Sharpton of their own.

"I want people who can go fight for us," says Wayne Ko, who runs the Korean Community Service Center of Brooklyn. "We have some inside Al Sharptons, but I want an Al Sharpton type of person to break outside."

This is, of course, a cultural impossibility—no one who acts like Al Sharpton would ever gain the respect of traditional Koreans. But many second-generation Korean-Americans—and the category known within the community as the "1.5 generation," people now in their teens, twenties, and thirties who came to America as children with their parents—say they are growing tired of marginality.

"A lot of people come here and feel overwhelmed to a point that they decide they want to insulate themselves from mainstream society," says Jonathan Kim, the nonprofit advocate, sitting in the Manhattan law office of his friend, Michael Yi. As Kim speaks, Yi nods sympathetically. But when it is suggested that the language gap stands in the way of assimilation—and that immi-

grants working seven-day weeks don't have time for English les-
sons—Yi responds with unusual bluntness: "They've been here
20, 30 years already. They don't have an excuse anymore."

Yi's snappishness reflects the growing exasperation the second
generation feels toward the first, a feeling returned by the elders,
who see their children defying them in the most awful ways.

The most extreme manifestation of Korean generational rebellion can sometimes be seen at the 109th Precinct station house
in Flushing. The parents stand there, waiting patiently for attention, the father red-faced, the mother crying into her hand.
They've come to report a missing child, or to collect a son, or even
a daughter, arrested for running with a gang. This is another way
in which the dynamic of the melting pot has changed: Assimilation is no longer the exalting process once imagined by fifties and
sixties liberals. For many morally upright immigrants, it now
means watching sons and daughters turn into miscreants, petty
criminals, or worse. "The families are just crushed," says William
Nevins, a police expert on Asian gangs.

The idea of Korean gangs defies all the stereotypes of Korean
diligence, but the gangs are there (if still in small numbers)—
Korean Fuk Ching, Korean Power, Korean-Taiwanese Boys—
robbing in Flushing and Elmhurst, extorting money from stores
in Koreatown in Manhattan. Even in Fort Lee, an Asian equivalent of Jewish Great Neck, the gangs troll successfully for initi-
ates, police say. They even reach the children of ministers, the
most respected members of the community. There is still a feeling
of disbelief in Queens, where the son of one of the community's
most prominent ministers was arrested in 1991 and later convicted for running with a gang of push-in robbers.

"These kids don't fit the typical profile," says Frank Hancock,
a criminal-defense attorney and gang expert. "You'll get a child at
the top of his class who comes from an industrious family, more
often than not in private business, working sixteen hours a day.
The problem is that these kids come home to an empty house.
The parents aren't aware of how trouble can creep up on you
here."

The Korean gangs take as models the larger Chinese gangs,
which they sometimes find themselves battling, as was the case in
1989, when gangs from Chinatown tried to shake down businesses along West 32nd Street, the heart of Manhattan's Koreatown. The Korean gangs, which had already locked up the extortion racket, posted sentries on the corners of Fifth Avenue and
32nd Street and fought off the Chinese interlopers.

No one is even guessing how many Korean businesses fall under the "protection" of gangs; Koreans, like many immigrant groups, are loath to involve the police in their affairs. But the man who led the Korean Power gang through the early nineties, Tony Kim, speaking to a reporter for the first time, provides a rare look into the world of renegade young Koreans.

"There are three kinds of extortions," he says, explaining the methods he employed. "One, basic robbery: 'You don't pay me money, I'll break you up.' The second is, 'I have people, young kids, in the gang, and I need to keep them off the streets, to get them food. You will give me money because I help them.' The third kind is police extortion: Police come; they want to arrest us; they threaten us. We were in the second kind of extortion."

Tony Kim came to America at the age of fourteen. At fifteen, he was charged with a robbery he says he didn't do. A leader of Korean Power, or KP, by the time he was sixteen, Kim worked the extortion business with becoming dedication.

"We do it the Korean way. We talk to the owner and say, 'You use our security; we work in your bar; maybe we could help keep other gangs from extorting you.' If they say, 'We didn't bring the money,' we'll go to [their] house with [them] to get the money. We'll even pay for the taxi. Sometimes they just see us as little brothers and want to give us something to eat, so they give us one, two hundred dollars."

The police, unsurprisingly, are less sanguine. "Five KP guys beat a guy up in his store just recently," Nevins says. "They told him that if he had security, this wouldn't happen. These are hard-core guys."

Tony Kim—ponytailed, scarred, and affable—says he's out of the gang life now and is running his new beeper business. He does not seem like a typical gang leader. Though he carries himself with the self-assurance of a person who knows his orders will be followed, he speaks deferentially and in complete sentences. He even apologizes for his fine English. And while he might be a nightmare vision to every Korean parent, Tony Kim expresses a degree of filial loyalty that Americans would find astonishing.

"When my father goes back to South Korea, I'll go back with him, give my time to him," he says, fiddling with his thumb ring. Right now, he's helping his father run the several dry cleaners the family owns in Queens. "My parents came here for a better life-style. For better education. Now they're thinking twice."

"We must fight the repressive mechanisms of the patriarchal world," the Reverend R. Yon Pak says as many of the sixty or so congregants nod in agreement. Many of them are in jeans; some have their ears pierced five or six times. One woman chews gum loudly as the minister speaks. "Before we came to America, my mother took us to visit our ancestral village, and there is a book there—this is my father's ancestral village—and it listed all the fathers and all the sons," she says. "My name wasn't in there."

There is a story in the Gospel according to Luke, Pak tells the congregation, of the "bent-over woman" who is miraculously cured of her ailments by Jesus, despite the opposition of the authorities at the time. Pak, a sunny-faced woman who speaks accented English, talks of the bent-over woman as an outcast, ignored and reviled by her community until Jesus sets her free. "We must not just believe in the suffering Christ or the glorified Christ but in the *confronting* Christ who never avoids social conflict."

For one in a Korean church especially, Pak's sermon is revolutionary. But the English Language Ministry of the Korean Methodist Church and Institute, near Columbia University, is catering to the assimilated. Across 115th Street, in a much larger hall, the Reverend Wontae Cha, a respected and senior Korean-American theologian, leads the same church's main service, in Korean.

Pak is a guest preacher, invited by Albert Hahn, the twenty-six-year-old minister to the English-language congregation. Pak was asked to speak this Sunday morning [Apr. 16] in honor of Women's History Month.

Cha, needless to say, is *not* celebrating Women's History Month. "We don't do that," he says, chuckling softly. "That street between us is very symbolic. Sometimes it's a barrier."

Back across the street, Hahn explains: "In the traditional Korean, Confucianist culture, God is the teacher, someone you look up to." Hahn is a soft-spoken, modest overachiever—Vassar, Princeton Theological Seminary. He arrived in America when he was fifteen. "That is how Koreans also perceive the pastor. When the pastor says something, that's the word. When people come to church, they are coming with respect. Korean-Americans see God as a friend we can relate to and admire but also complain to. It's a different outlook."

The cherubic Hahn is asked whether Cha and his supporters like what he is doing. "They pay my salary," he replies coolly.

Cha's congregants would almost certainly be displeased by what happens later in Hahn's service. A woman in her mid-twenties gets up to introduce her new fiancé, who is white. The congregation cheers. It's a willful denial of the hard feelings interracial marriages engender in more conservative parts of the Korean community.

Curiously, both ministers describe themselves as adherents of liberation theology, placing them to the left of the mass of Korean ministers in New York. Hahn speaks of the "diseases of capitalism" and analyzes Korean-black tensions in quasi-Marxist language. "The problems between Koreans and blacks are set up by the racist system," he says.

This is a rarity. Churches keep the community glued together, but they rarely conceive of their mission in political terms. Though more than 60 percent of Koreans in the New York area describe themselves as Christian, an even higher percentage attend one of the region's 500 Korean churches. Many go just for the opportunity to socialize with their fellow émigrés. To the extent that ideology comes up at all, most churches encourage a brand of apolitical conservatism, Cha says. "They don't teach them how democracy is a part of Christianity."

Michael Yi, the lawyer and activist, puts it more confrontationally: "It would be against the interests of the ministers to make these people part of society. 'Keep them alienated from mainstream society' is the thinking."

Of the political issues that divide young Koreans from their parents, race is where the understanding gap may be the widest. American-born Koreans tell of their shame at the things their parents sometimes say about blacks. None would humiliate their parents by speaking for attribution.

"In Korea, the image of blacks isn't positive," one young professional says. "My parents came over with an image of blacks as violent, and then they hear about the problems their friends have with blacks in the stores. They basically think they're scary. They think they have a low mentality."

Blacks and Koreans were, of course, destined for trouble. The relationship began in the early sixties, when Korean wig sellers started visiting Harlem to sell thick Korean hair, which was then popular in black beauty salons. Louis Winnick, a researcher with the Fund for the City of New York, says that the Koreans noticed a large number of empty stores, many freshly abandoned by Jewish merchants. The Koreans moved in, graduating from wigs to dry goods and produce. The rest is strife-torn history. "Shoplifting black dollars" is the headline on a recent story about Korean merchants in *Emerge* magazine, the usually solid black monthly that on this issue decided to let the raw antipathy fly.

Wayne Ko, a round, slightly befuddled man with a mission to

reform his community, says he understands the sentiments behind these racialist feelings. "I tell my people, 'Do not think all the
time about money,'" Ko says. He's seated at a table in a Blimpie
restaurant on Flatbush Avenue. "We should learn more about"—
he looks around and drops his voice to a whisper—"black
people." The coast is clear. "We have to learn the customs in the
black neighborhoods."

It was tried before, with mixed success. Part of the problem is
cultural—Korean society is so reserved that during the 1988
Olympics, radio and television announcements reminded residents of Seoul to smile at strangers. When Confucian coolness
collides with "How ya doin'" American openness, the results can
be dangerous.

"In Korea, we can't smile too much; it looks insincere," Ko
says. "It's the way we grow up. But we should learn to smile."

In Korean society, too, women seldom look men, especially
strangers, in the eye. To do so would be to express extreme emotion. Here, though, averted eyes behind the counter can signify
disrespect, especially to people looking for slights. In the Korean-
owned stores along Flatbush Avenue and in the grocery store that
was the focus of the 1990 boycott, the merchants seem to be
Americanizing their customs. They put money directly into the
customers' hands—in Korea, money is customarily placed on the
counter—and they smile and say thank you. One recent afternoon, though, a broom-wielding employee vigilantly followed a
young black woman through one store, his body language sug-
gesting that he expected the woman to grab something and run.
She quickly left, and the employee, gripping the broom tightly,
mumbled, "Always stealing, always stealing."

In Chang-rae Lee's *Native Speaker,* the narrator recalls the way
his father, a taciturn shopkeeper, reacted to blacks: "With blacks
he just turned to stone. He never bothered to explain his prices to
them. He didn't follow them around the aisles like some store-
keepers do, but he always let them know there wasn't going to be
any *funny business* here. When a young black man or woman came
in—old people or those with children in tow didn't seem to alarm
him—he took his broom and started sweeping at the store entrance very slowly, deliberately, not looking at the floor."

Few blacks come into the O-Bok Oriental Food store on Hillel
Place in Flatbush. None are apparently working here, which is no
surprise, since Koreans say privately that they believe blacks make
poor workers—Mexicans appear to be the employees of choice.

In fact, it's lucky for the Koreans that few blacks come into the store: They'd be unamused by a display of Kalahari-brand Korean tea, planted right by the door, that features a drawing of a black man with a bone through his nose. The store is a haven for Koreans in the area; it's a wholesaler that sells mostly Korean food, so it's a safe place for a group of store owners to talk about race without worrying who's around.

The men, their hands brown with work, pour one another sake and steel themselves for unpleasant talk.

Michael Lee, a normally voluble produce wholesaler, turns grave when he's asked to describe race relations from his perspective. "Four times I was robbed," he says. "Two times by three men and two times by two men. All black. After that, every time a black man opens the front of his jacket, I am scared. I have to think there are good black men and bad black men. The black man who caught the crazy man who pushed the old Korean lady onto the subway tracks—he was a good black man. I don't think Koreans have . . ." He loses the word. Much discussion in Korean. "*Bias*. I don't think Koreans have bias." He takes a pen and writes the word on his hand, to remind himself.

Another grocer offers up his theory on black shoplifting. It's wildly, preposterously racist, but not without a trace of first-stage empathy. "The blacks pick apples and bananas from the store," he says. "A long time ago, in the fields, the blacks took food off the trees, so this is why they take apples and bananas. Sometimes they forget not to take fruit." His statement leads to an extended discussion about declining banana prices.

"We need to understand the black people better," says Michael Lee, waving his bias hand. "I don't want to hurt other people, and I don't want to get hurt."

Outside, the sun is setting as hundreds of people stream out of the Flatbush Avenue subway station. The few Koreans caught in the crowd of tired black workers keep their heads down and move swiftly, as if they're trying to beat their own shadows to safety.

The four undergraduate women who make up the Columbia University Korean Modern Hip-Hop Dance troupe take the stage at Korean Culture Night 1995. Their friends hoot in delight as their elders sit in confusion. According to the culture-night program handout, the hip-hop dancers were booted out of the Korean fan-dance group at Columbia for engaging in what the group disapprovingly called "outrageous dance antics." They decided to form the new group to demonstrate "how to be young, hip, and Korean."

There are maybe 500 students in the ballroom, all young, nearly all Korean, and quite a few unhip, though not for lack of trying. The boys, gangly and intense, keep their bangs long and wear string ties; others dress as if they're heading to Wall Street interviews right after curtain call. The women, more self-assured, glide through the room in sleek and expensive black dresses.

The program this Saturday night is a celebration of Korean culture, and a statement of Korean permanency at Columbia. The 500-member Korean Students Association has rented for the evening one of Columbia's largest ballrooms. Tonight is a chance for students who otherwise lead textbook American lives to remind themselves who they are, though they tend to do this in the generationally correct style. After one student finishes playing ancient folk music on a *kayagum*, similar to the Japanese *koto*, a student emcee sneers that "every time I hear the *kayagum*, I get so emotional." In case you missed the irony the first time around, she begins to sniffle into the microphone.

The hip-hoppers are greeted more enthusiastically. "Go girls!" someone in the audience screams.

But the hip-hoppers seem acutely self-conscious, and they smirk as the music—edge-free, watery Korean pop—reverbs through the room. Dressed in baggy jeans, Pumas, and bandannas, they make a stab at rump-shaking. This homage to black street culture is yet another (if more benign) manifestation of the new melting pot. But this is no booty video in the making. After the show, many students say they're going home to study.

Theirs is an uneasy rebellion. Most of the kids in this hall, after all, came to Columbia smothered in a blanket of responsibility. "Growing up, you know the air you breathe in your house is not free," John Min, the premed student, says. "When your parents come home at night, you know they weren't out at clubs. They come home and they can't put food in their mouths fast enough, and then they go to sleep so they can wake up six hours later to go back to work. They're not working sixteen hours a day to get a Mercedes. There's easier ways to get a Mercedes. Their blood, sweat, and tears fund the success of the next generation. It's not luxury they're looking for."

Second-generation Koreans tell astounding stories of their parents' obsession with the Ivy League. Marie Lee, a Brown-educated fiction writer, tells how her father wrote away for Harvard applications on the days each of his three children were born. "When my oldest brother got into Harvard, my father was in Turkey, so he bought a Muslim prayer rug in celebration," she says. Universities do not break down admissions statistics by Asian nationality, but educated guesses from Columbia, Yale, and Harvard student leaders place the proportion of Koreans in those schools at about 5 percent. Korean-Americans make up less than one percent of the total U.S. population.

The Korean commitment to education cannot be overestimated. "The majority of Koreans immediately want to move out to Long Island," says Su Yong Choi, a onetime grocery-store owner in the city who now lives on Long Island and owns a shirt factory in the Dominican Republic. "First comes Flushing, then Bayside, then Long Island. It is because the Korean is like the Jews in education. We want to send our children to the schools the Jews go to."

It's the Northern Boulevard Express, the trek of Koreans out of Flushing into Long Island's North Shore, to communities with the best high schools. Ranking high schools is apparently a perennial exercise among successful Korean immigrants, if Su Yong Choi is typical. "First Great Neck North, then Great Neck South, then Herricks, and Hewlett and Syosset. Roslyn is so-so," he says, counting down. Many Koreans say they pay particular attention to the number of students from each school accepted by the Ivies. Obviously, not all second-generation Koreans land in graduate school. There are special pressures for those who neither drop out entirely nor excel. Few Korean parents want to see their children follow them into small business, even if the child shows an ability to make a business grow. Susie Rhim is one such case. She is the Susie of Susie's Kitchen, a sprawling new deli and salad bar on Park Avenue South, near 30th Street. Susie is 27 and runs the deli with her mother, Koh Ja Rhim, and her father, Soon Il Rhim. Susie has a younger sister, Helen, at Brown University.

Her mother, who runs a cash register, was trained to be a violinist at Seoul National University. Her father, whose specialty now is spotting shoplifters, studied literature at Yonsei. It is the end of the day; the lunch rush is over, and the Rhims uncomplainingly hide their fatigue.

Why did they go into the deli business?

"Do you know what it costs to go to Brown University?" Soon Il asks.

"Twenty thousand dollars a year?"

"No." He shakes his head.

"Twenty-five thousand a year?"

"No," he says again, his voice filling with pride.

"Thirty thousand a year?"

"*More* than $30,000 a year."

Though Susie and Helen are only eight years apart, the Rhims talk about them as if they are from different generations, and they are. Susie vividly recalls her family's struggles. "I remember being woken up in the middle of the night to go to the market. I remember ripening avocados in the apartment," she says. By the time Helen was born, the Rhims had turned their ghetto grocery store into a going concern (they left Williamsburg in 1974 for Manhattan). "They didn't have money to send me to tennis camp like they did with Helen," Susie says, showing no resentment.

Susie, who attended Boston University and then New York University, but didn't graduate, seems happy with the choices she's made. She's engaged to a Southerner named Patrick Nation, who helps manage the store. Susie's parents seem pleased with Patrick and happy with her work in the new store, but not overjoyed. "She'll finish school," her father declares.

It's hard to imagine, sometimes, why a violinist and a man who loves literature chose to spend their days chopping vegetables and chasing shoplifters. Can a child's education cancel out everything?

Chang-rae Lee, the novelist, says that for many parents, their personal pleasure is irrelevant. "I guess they would say that the suffering is not an issue; there's no need to talk about that," he says. "'Why complain if my children's lives are better?'"

But the children worry nonetheless. The weight of their parents' sacrifice can be crushing. Sitting in a Sizzler by the water in Sheepshead Bay one Saturday afternoon, Henry Jung admits that he could never find the courage to ask his mother whether she now regrets her decision to come to America.

"It's a very good question, but I don't want to ask," he says. "I'm afraid of the answer."

II. THE IMMIGRATION FLOW ACROSS THE MEXICO-U.S. BORDER

EDITOR'S INTRODUCTION

The articles in this section deal with immigrants coming to America across the Mexican border. No aspect of the immigration debate has stirred such controversy, particularly since illegal border crossings have doubled in recent times, at present running to about 500,000 a year. The three thousand mile length of the frontier between the two countries makes it virtually impossible to intercept all crossings; and because of a lack of prison space, those who *are* apprehended are returned to Mexico, where they will try their luck again. The question posed in this section is how the influx of these illegals ought to be regarded. Do they represent a threat to the stability of the United States that requires some drastic action, or can they, after all, be accommodated?

A revealing article by Douglas Payne in *Harper's*, which opens Section Two, examines that social and economic conditions in Mexico that spur immigrant flight to the north. Payne describes the *ciudades perdidas*, or "lost cities," that spread across the volcanic floor of the Valley of Mexico and constitute the biggest slum in North America. Here young men under the age of twenty, who make up a surprisingly large percentage of the population, have no employment and no future. Their illegal flight northward in search of a better life is predictable, and the Mexican government does not work very hard to prevent it: the exodus relieves the unemployment problem, and the remittances sent home to Mexico add at least two billion dollars annually to that country's economy. In the following article, reprinted from *Dissent*, Richard Rothstein weighs the pros and cons of immigration from Mexico, noting that while the immigrants do compete for some jobs with American citizens, sometimes also pushing down the wage scale, they also add significantly to the economy by filling jobs in farming and the garment industry, and working for low wages in jobs that Americans are unwilling to take.

To presidential aspirant Patrick Buchanan, in a March 1995 campaign address in New Hampshire there are no two ways of thinking about the surge of illegal immigration from Mexico. He is entirely opposed to it and would construct a steel shield along the border, bringing in the National Guard to reinforce the Border Patrol. Buchanan intends to make immigration a major issue in his political campaign for the 1996 election. Next, David Corn, writing in *The Nation,* unleashes a scathing attack on Buchanan as a fear-mongering extremist with prejudicial views of foreigners, particularly Hispanics. In the section's final piece, reprinted from *America,* Peter A. Quinn takes up the question of racist fears of white America, which have often been raised by the presence of new immigrants. He describes on the campaign of the eugenicists in the wake of the First World War to halt the tide of immigration from southern and eastern Europe. He also notes a similarly alarmed response to the "famine Irish" who poured into America in the 1850s. It would be well, Quinn concludes, to see in the "faces of today's immigrants the image of our ancestors: those hungry ghosts who, though dispossessed and despised, passed on to us their faith and their hope."

MEXICO AND ITS DISCONTENTS[1]

Last winter, in New York, I watched the televised panic on the floor of the Bolsa, the Mexican stock exchange, and as I listened to a reporter describe the collapse of the peso and the threats to free trade with Latin America, I found myself thinking of the Mexicans I had come to know the previous summer in the *ciudades perdidas,* or "lost cities," the slums that spread, lava-like, across the volcanic floor of the Valley of Mexico. When you are standing in a lost city, the towers of Mexico City's downtown can only occasionally be glimpsed as they rise like the masts of a derelict treasure fleet through the shallow sea of smog that drowns the capital. In today's global economy, it is often said, the mobility of money prevents investors from having to live with the consequences of their actions. In the case of Mexico, however, the mobility of people may ensure that the investors will person-

[1]Article by Douglas W. Payne, Latin American and Caribbean specialist at Freedom House in New York, from *Harper's* 290:68–74 Ap '95. Copyright © 1995 by *Harper's Magazine.* All rights reserved. Reprinted with permission.

ally confront the consequences of their mistakes, and as I watched the news from the Bolsa, I wondered how many residents of the lost cities of Mexico soon would be gazing up through another haze at the iridescent spires of Wall Street.

In January, as the peso crisis played out, the White House warned that if the Mexican economy collapsed, as many as five hundred thousand illegal immigrants would cross the border this year. And, in fact, that same month the number of illegal immigrants apprehended along the U.S.-Mexican border doubled. Despite the Clinton Administration's effort to strengthen the border patrol, it remains easy for illegal immigrants to cross. The Mexican government has consistently refused to cooperate in tightening the common border—to no one's surprise. After all, the greatest open secret in U.S.-Mexican relations (apart from the marriage of convenience between drug traffickers and much of the Mexican establishment) is Mexico's tacit support of illegal immigration.

When then Mexican president Carlos Salinas barnstormed the United States during the NAFTA showdown, he argued that the free-trade agreement would create jobs, lift Mexican wages, and thereby keep more Mexicans at home. It was an appealing tune, and NAFTA proponents in the United States performed variations on the refrain. Independent Mexican economists, however, have suggested that the annual informal immigration to the United States of hundreds of thousands, if not millions, of Mexicans is part of the strategic economic planning of Mexico's political elites. If true, no government official would confess to the idea because of the political firestorm it would create, especially given the ruckus over California's Proposition 187. It is telling, though, that the Mexican government opposed the California ballot measure designed to deny illegal immigrants most state-government services.

Salinas came close to admitting the obvious when he told *New Perspectives Quarterly,* "I am for the free movement of labor." Needless to say, he was not referring to the migration of American workers giving up five-dollar-an-hour jobs in Detroit to work in *maquiladoras* ("factories") in Sonora or Tamaulipas for five dollars a day. He was thinking of many, if not most, of Mexico's poor, who, from the point of view of the Mexican government, are dead weight—that is, unless they send money home after crossing the only contiguous border between a Third World country and a First World country (when Mexico acquired "First World" creden-

tials in 1994, upon being accepted as the twenty-fifth member of
the Organization for Economic Cooperation and Development
[OECD], no one was fooled except gullible foreign investors).
Already an estimated 10 percent of Mexico's population, or nine
to ten million Mexicans, now live in the United States, and many
of them send money south. The Mexican central bank calculates
that dollar remittances to Mexico top $2 billion annually; inde-
pendent studies indicate that the figure is actually higher. The
remittances are now the third largest source of hard currency for
Mexico, after oil and tourism.

Illegal immigration is important not only as a source of cash
flowing into the Mexican economy but also as an outlet for Mexico's overflowing population. The country has seen a 23 percent
population growth in the last ten years, to ninety-two million.
Even in the past few years, when Salinastroika had appeared to be
working, the poor of Mexico saw little chance for upward mobility
in a society in which 54 percent of the nation's wealth was controlled by 20 percent of the population, including twenty-four
Forbes-certified billionaires (reduced to ten after the devaluation,
according to *Forbes*). The Mexican government reports that national joblessness is between 3 and 4 percent, but by its criteria
someone begging on the street is employed. Some analysts estimate that the unemployment rate is actually up to eight times
higher and that as many as 40 percent of workers are toiling in
the informal economy. Those lucky enough to be employed in the
formal sector have suffered as well: from 1982 to 1994 wages lost
about 60 percent of their real buying power. It was largely by
suppressing wages that the Salinas government cut inflation from
above 150 percent annually in 1987 to about 7 percent in 1994.
From 1988 to 1994 the minimum wage was allowed to rise only
from about $3.85 a day to $4.60. When, last December, the few
pesos in their pockets lost almost half their value overnight, poor
Mexicans suddenly had a much greater incentive to go north.

Now that remittances in dollars are much more valuable, and
the Mexican poor even more desperate, President Ernesto
Zedillo, like his predecessor, will surely be in favor of "the free
movement of labor." When all its other methods of social control
fail, the Mexican government has a ready safety valve: the lost
cities of Mexico are only about five hundred miles from Browns-
ville, Texas.

"It's as though they *want* us to go," Emilio, a street vendor, told
me during my visit to the lost cities last August, at the time of the

presidential election. The denizens of the *ciudades perdidas*, though, need little encouragement from the government to leave; it would be a wonder if anyone who had a choice wanted to dwell a day longer amid the squalor of the biggest slum in North America.

The oldest and largest of the lost cities is Nezahualcóyotl. Named after an Aztec poet–warrior prince whose name means "ravenous coyote," "Neza," as it is commonly known, may itself be the third most populous municipality in Mexico, after the capital and Guadalajara. Neza began in the late 1940s as a squatter settlement of a few thousand near the Mexico City airport, at a time when the capital's poor lived mostly in cramped downtown barrios. But as Mexico's industrialization made the city a mecca for millions of unemployed rural workers, what was once a manageable community exploded. The original boundaries of the capital, the Federal District, were obliterated as Greater Mexico City oozed across the floor of the 7,400-foot-high valley in Mexico's central plateau and into the surrounding state of Mexico to become a megalopolis of more than twenty-two million people.

Saturated by the rural exodus, Neza spilled over to the east and south into the burgeoning slums of Chimalhuacán, La Paz, and Chalco. Now Neza hugs the swampy remains of Lake Texcoco, an ecological wasteland at the very bottom of the Valley of Mexico. Before Neza crept to its shores, the lake served as the primary receptacle for Mexico City's sewage and industrial wastes. It still does. The facility built to treat and pump the waste out of the valley is overwhelmed. In the rainy season (May to October) the *aguas negras*, or "black waters," overflow into Neza's grid-patterned streets. They feed pond-size, insect-spawning pools that leach into wells, contaminate Neza's chronically inadequate supply of potable water, and on occasion spew a toxic soup into homes. In the dry season, prevailing northwest winds churn up storms of fecal dust.

At first glance, Neza and the other *ciudades perdidas* remind a visitor of other Third World megacities. There are the same unpaved streets choked with mud, trash, and human waste; the swarms of battered Bluebird buses and rusted minivans packed with people, animals, and goods; the seemingly endless expanses of cement and scrap-metal shanties; the children whose knees buckle from hunger as they walk; the dazed looks of the chronically ill; the joblessness; the alcohol; the drugs; and the packs of stray dogs. But Mexico's lost cities are different from the *favelas* of Rio de Janeiro—where drug traffickers, police, and the Brazilian

army battle for turf in what Brazilian President Fernando Henri-
que Cardoso has described as "undeclared civil war"—and distinct, as well, from the seething hillside barrios of Caracas—
where feral youth gangs own the night and the police show up
only during daylight to number the corpses. Mexico's lost cities
display a unique form of order, imposed by the Mexican oligarchy through time-tested mechanisms of social and political
control.

I saw a manifestation of that control in the metal garbage carts
pulled by horses and donkeys that streamed in and out of an
enormous lakeside dump in Neza. The carts were painted with a
logo in green, white, and red. These are Mexico's national colors.
They are also colors usurped by the Institutional Revolutionary
Party (PRI), the world's longest ruling political party, incorporated as Mexico's state party in 1929.

On top of the mounds of refuse, beyond the horse-drawn
carts, a small army of *pepenadores*, or scavengers—men, women,
children—were systematically digging for glass, metal, wood,
newsprint, or anything else that could be sold to the lords of the
dump, the PRI *cacique* and his heavies (*cacique*, meaning "boss," is
the old Nahua Indian word for village chief). In all the giant
dumps that have risen like volcanoes amid the lost cities, the
pepenadores have been tightly organized by the PRI. At election
time, they vote en masse for the party; for PRI political rallies or
May Day parades, they are often hauled in like produce on
trucks. In exchange, they are allowed to live on the dump in
hovels constructed from materials they have scavenged and to
make their living by sifting through the garbage. Rafael Gutiérrez
Moreno, the late "Garbage King" who once presided over an
array of lost-city dumps, amassed such wealth and power selling
recyclable materials and delivering the votes of the *pepenadores*
that in 1979 he won election as an alternate to Mexico's federal
legislature.

The regimentation of the *pepenadores* is but one of the blatant
manifestations of the PRI's continuing control over the lives of
Mexico City's poor. Consider the experiences of Feliciana, who
lives on a pothole-pitted side street near Colonia Maravillas, one
of Neza's older sections. With deep lines in her face and graying
hair pulled back into a braid, she appears to be in her sixties. She
and her late husband and their three small children came from
the state of Puebla in the late 1950s and built a house on a tiny
plot purchased from a real estate company that advertised a

bountiful new life in Maravillas ("Marvels"). They soon discovered, however, that the land was not the company's to sell when a *cacique* showed up with the police and threatened to have them and their neighbors evicted if they did not ante up protection money. "We had to pay," Feliciana told me. "If we didn't pay him, he'd stop the water trucks from coming. There was nothing here then: no streets, no electricity, nothing. It was a desert. We couldn't live without water."

In a landscape as nightmarish as one of Salvador Dali's icon-littered deserts, families like Feliciana's have constructed their own homes from cinder block, corrugated metal, and scrap wood. Over the years many have added on extra rooms and second stories in order to house expanding or extended families, or to rent to newcomers as the land ran out (the residents of Neza are now packed some 150,000 to a square mile). Feliciana described the decades-long struggle that the community waged to get the government to provide land titles and install basic services. "Once there were enough of us, they wanted our votes," she said. "Then we got some things. But only if we supported the PRI,"

The oligarchy is insatiable. Feliciana pays taxes on her property and taxes for utilities, one fee to the city to operate her store and another, evidently a monthly shakedown, to the neighborhood *cacique*. What is left of her profits from the soft drinks, candies, and cosmetics she sells in her store—a small shed next to the two-room house she shares with a daughter and four grandchildren—plus the meager earnings from the sewing her daughter takes in, barely keeps the household in beans and tortillas.

"We are always paying," she said. "The PRI, it is a mafia."

As the lost cities grow, so does the control of the PRI. In the newer slum of Chalco the poorest of the lost-city poor are rapidly populating another ancient lake bed, presided over by Popocatépetl and Ixtaccíhuatl, two volcanoes that, in Mexican folklore, were once human lovers. In 1519 the Spaniard Hernán Cortés marched his army through the high pass between the peaks on his way to conquer the Aztecs.

Today, Chalco is being conquered by the PRI. I visited there for a few days, and on the ride out along the Mexico-Puebla highway, a young woman with Mayan features fell asleep against my shoulder on the crowded bus. She was awakened by the miasma emitted from a garbage dump cut into a hillside along the road. The *pepenadores* there had used rocks, painted white, to spell out "COLOSIO" in huge letters along the slope, in homage

to Luis Donaldo Colosio, the PRI presidential candidate assassi-
nated five months before.

The woman's name was Imelda. She told me she had a clean-
ing job in the capital that paid a minimum wage, then $4.60 per
day, a quarter of which was eaten up by the cost of her daily, five-
hour round-trip commute. Her husband, a day laborer, had to
pay dues to a PRI-controlled construction union to be able to
work; even so, his employment was sporadic. Imelda's greatest
concern, however, was holding on to their still unfinished house
in one of Chalco's newest settlements, miles from a paved road.

As Imelda and I trudged through the mud toward her home,
a tiny box of cement and brick, she told me that a few days earlier
the police had come to the settlement and threatened to throw
everyone out because the people from whom they purchased
their parcels of land had defrauded them. Then representatives
from the PRI arrived and told them that their sales receipts were
worthless but that they would receive help in obtaining title to the
land if they promised to vote for the PRI the following Sunday.
"My husband and I told them we understood," she said. "What
choice did we have? We have no place else to go. We have children.
But I heard that others around here protested. I'm afraid of what
might happen."

Buttoned-down PRI spokesmen in the capital like to say the
caciques are a thing of the past. But Imelda's story was nearly
identical to Feliciana's, only it was happening now in Chalco. And
in Chimalhuacán, another new slum, a group of women gathered
around me down the street from a polling station. "They tell us if
we don't vote for the PRI, we won't be allowed to register our
children in school," one of them said, her fists clenched at her
side. "That is against the law." The Mexican constitution, in fact,
guarantees not only free primary education but also adequate
housing for all Mexicans. When I said the vote was supposed to be
secret, they all shook their heads. "Look, mister," one of them
said, "if the PRI is not satisfied with the number of votes they get
here, then everybody here will pay the price. They control everything."

Having listened to many similar tales of political extortion in
the weeks preceding the August election, before leaving Mexico I
tipped off Mark Fineman, Mexico City bureau chief for the *Los
Angeles Times*. A few weeks after the election, Fineman went to
Chalco and found 420 families huddled in an unfinished prima-
ry-school building. They had been threatened just as the people

in Imelda's settlement had been. Evidently they had refused to kowtow to the bosses. Hundreds of municipal riot police had rousted them, demolished their shanties, and robbed many of them of their belongings. Ignacio Martínez Romero, the school's director, had offered temporary refuge. He told Fineman, as quoted in the *Los Angeles Times* (September 17, 1994), "Everything here is (about) land . . . and fraud is the system. At this level, fraud and politics seem to go together."

The sentiment was echoed by Marcelino, a gardener and fix-it man in a hillside community near Neza called Loma Encantada ("Enchanted Hill"). "The government manipulates the poverty of the people," he said. "The government is the father and we are supposed to be the children. If we do not behave we are punished." Marcelino was giving me his view of Solidarity, the multi-billion-dollar program initiated by Salinas to combat poverty in a country that has neither unemployment benefits nor a welfare system. Solidarity is described by the government as a politically neutral, self-help program in which citizens form local commit-tees to determine what are the most pressing needs—a school, a well, electricity. "Here, the *caciques* control these committees and they control the money," Marcelino told me. "Most of us here on this hill oppose the government. And you see what we have—nothing." On the other side of Loma Encantada there recently had been a Solidarity ceremony for the opening of a new soccer field. "Those people there are hungry. Do you really believe that was their decision, to build a soccer field? What's more, that field was built by a company owned by a PRI-ista. So you see where the money went in the end."

The Solidarity officials I encountered in the lost cities all de-nied that there was any political pressure involved with the Soli-darity program. I spoke to one official (who if named would be punished by the PRI) as he inspected a foul-smelling drainage ditch in the Covadonga settlement in Chalco, which is known as the cradle of Solidarity because it is where Carlos Salinas himself came to inaugurate the program (the electrical system that Salinas promised Chalco was eventually installed, but it then cost about $270 to hook up to it, more than three times what a minimum-wage earner makes in a month). "Look," the official said, "the real problem is that many people here don't understand how we are trying to help them. They must participate more." After taking a call on a walkie-talkie he excused himself. Across the road he stepped into a new four-wheel-drive Solidarity vehicle. As he drove away I noticed PRI campaign posters with the face of presidential candidate Ernesto Zedillo pasted to the sides.

Any contemplation of Mexico's future must account for the fact that half the population is under the age of twenty. In Neza the figure is closer to 60 percent. With the cost of secondary school beyond the reach of most families, the alternatives are limited minimum-wage jobs, unemployment, gangs, hanging out.

Unlike many of his peers, Hector, at the age of eighteen, had found a way to make money in the underground *rocanrol* business. I came upon his stall in a street market near Colonia Evolución. A group of longhaired *chavos* ("young toughs") in denim and leather jackets were browsing through hundreds of bootleg cassettes. All were hard rock—traditional, heavy-metal, thrash, punk. They were by U.S. and European bands, and by home-grown Mexican bands too. Silk-screened T-shirts for sale quilted the cavelike stall. "Hand of Doom" by Black Sabbath blared from Hector's Panasonic boom box.

Hector told me his big sellers included "anything metal," the Doors, the Sex Pistols, and the Ramones, whose likeness appeared on his shirt. Grunge, he said, holding up a Nirvana tape, was beginning to catch on. He explained that he bought cassettes from dealers in the capital, then made duplicates on his boom box to sell at a price the locals could afford. He also received cassettes in the mail from a cousin in Chicago, but had to give "tips" to postal workers to keep them from stealing his packages.

A lot of Mexico's underground rock, which thrives in working-class barrios, is an expression of rage—against the government, industrial pollution, the rich, the police. You will not hear it on Mexican radio. Some bands revel in impending doom—civil war, environmental disaster, nuclear holocaust. Others espouse a neo-anarchism that calls for total war against authority—governmental, parental, or religious. Hector said that years ago the government used to crack down on the scene. "But then it wised up," he added. "The kids just want to get wasted, they don't want to be Zapatistas."

I knew that Neza had spawned a particularly virulent strain of rock, and I asked Hector about Los Mierdas Punk ("The Punk Shits"), one of Neza's first *punkero* groups. He said he heard they had broken up, but he had a number of cassettes by Neza's newer breeds, some of which he had taped himself at live concerts. Los Desviados ("The Deviates"), snarling speed metal. Colectiva Caó-

tica, straight punk. And Desobediencia Civil, growling thrash.
Here are some of the latter's lyrics, as best as I can make them out:

> . . . *You can't live*
> *You can't think*
> *As long as the government exists*
> *They make you sick*
> *They make you empty*
> *They kill you if you won't die* . . .

That night I went with Hector to Salón Cinco ("Room Five"), a
walled-in, roofless parking lot off Avenida Lopez Mateos, a wide
street that runs north-south through Neza. Hector explained that
rockero entrepreneurs far bigger than he rented parking lots or
closed off an alley for a night and paid off the *caciques* and the
police to put on events. "These things are never announced,"
Hector said. "Word gets passed on the streets."

The throb of rock music could be heard blocks away. We paid
ten pesos apiece, were frisked by a gauntlet of bouncers, then
elbowed our way in. At the end of the long rectangular lot two
shirtless D.J.s with ponytails swayed over a console on an elevated
platform. Big black speakers stacked along the cinder-block walls
brought forth a song called *"Tus días están contados"* ("Your Days
Are Numbered") by Transmetal, a band from Ecatepec, an industrial area across Lake Texcoco. Sheets of orange tarp ballooned
above a floor teeming with two thousand kids in *rockero* regalia—
black leather jackets and vests, jeans, miniskirts, safety pins. A
number of teens had woven into sweatshirts and caps U.S. team
logos: the Dallas Cowboys and the Los Angeles Raiders. Some
kids danced, some posed, others shared joints or clear plastic bags
of beer. The most popular intoxicant, at least among the *chavos*,
seemed to be industrial solvents, which they poured from metal
cans onto balled cotton or cloth held in their hands, then inhaled
through their fists. Under a set of wooden stairs, dozens of them
had fallen into a stupor.

I followed Hector up the stairs to a narrow catwalk from
which I could look out over the wall. The street lights of Neza
rippled into the distance across the floor of the Valley of Mexico.
Below, an old woman in a white dress with a shawl covering her
head entered one of the fifteen or so cubicles that ringed a cramped courtyard.

Hector tugged my arm, drawing my attention back inside.
Some speed-metal song by a Mexican band I could not identify

was playing. In front of the thundering speakers, hundreds of kids were jumping and whirling in a tight oval formation while others tried to hurl themselves on top.

Two days later I stood outside the Neza Stadium, an oval hulk of concrete moated by stagnant water that filled the depressions in its buckled parking lot. I had come for a look because I had heard that the stadium was slowly listing into the soft lake bed and that the Neza Toros soccer club had to play all their matches away from home. From behind I heard, "Hey, friend," in English and turned to see a young man jump off a bus and head toward me. His curly black hair hung to his shoulders. He wore madras Bermuda shorts, dirt-caked cowboy boots, and a tight-fitting sleeveless T-shirt with "Metallica" emblazoned across the front.

"You are from over there, right?" he asked me, "over there" being his English translation of *el otro lado,* "the other side." His name, he said, was Gustavo, and it turned out that he had crossed illegally into the United States in 1988 and had been a member of a gang in East Los Angeles. He had spent a few years in a California youth facility for attempted murder—"Gang-banging, you know." Then he had been deported. Now nineteen and back in Neza, he worked for the minimum wage making change on the bus he had just gotten off. I asked him about the stadium. "Sure, it's sinking," he said, switching into Spanish. "Man, everything here is sinking. What's *chingón* ("fucking great") is that the new jail is sinking, too."

It was late on a Sunday afternoon and Gustavo and a friend, Andres, heavyset, a few years older, were done for the day. Gustavo wanted me to see the jail. Andres was more interested in asking about New York. How cold is it? There are Mexicans there, right? What kinds of work can you find? Are there a lot of blonde women?

As we drove down Avenida Rancho Grande, Andres swerved back and forth to avoid the horse-drawn garbage carts wobbling toward the lakeside dumps, the dogs that snapped after them, and the craters in the road. Gustavo wanted to know if I was afraid of getting robbed. There are hundreds of youth gangs in Neza, and many older residents had told me they do not go out at night.

"They're not so tough, really, not like in L.A., where everybody has guns." He said he was more wary of the police. "The cops are the real criminals here. They work for the politicos. You know, harassing people. They put you in jail for nothing, then they steal your money, your clothes, everything."

The new jail, an enormous flat concrete structure, had been built out on Lake Texcoco amid the dumps. Razor wire scrolled along the top of its gray walls. But the twelve pillbox towers guarded no one; the structure was empty. I later found out that the prison, like the stadium, was indeed sinking into the marsh, but that engineers hoped to solve the problem in time for it to open later this year. "Look at that thing, man," Gustavo said. "You can put a lot of *chavos* in there."

A passenger jet ascended from the airport and climbed out over the lake. Andres asked me how long it took to fly to New York.

IMMIGRATION DILEMMAS[2]

During the presidential campaign, Bill Clinton delivered a foreign policy speech in Los Angeles; the first question from the audience was a predictable, "Who are your foreign policy advisers going to be?" Clinton demurred, calling such considerations premature. Next, a questioner asked the candidate what he proposed to do about illegal immigration. Clinton said he didn't know what to do, since immigration was the most complex issue facing the nation. "If you have an answer," Clinton told the questioner, "*you* can be my foreign policy adviser!" It may have been the first time the "policy-wonk" candidate couldn't come up with a ready solution.

The impossibility of border control is the most obvious difficulty. The Coast Guard can't effectively police every mile of our coastline; the occasional interception of a Chinese human cargo ship is only token. We now have over three thousand federal agents patrolling two thousand miles of the U.S.-Mexican land border, also with little success. Last year, the border patrol intercepted 1.2 million would-be immigrants from Mexico, but since

[2]Article by Richard Rothstein, writer on labor, education, and immigration, from *Dissent* 40:455–62 Fall '93. Copyright © 1993 by *Dissent*. Reprinted with permission.

there is no point to incarcerating them (or jail space to do so),
nearly all are sent back to try again; 100,000 to 600,000 a year
evade capture. So if the intercepted ones keep trying, the odds
are increasingly in their favor.

Giving up on border control is no solution either. Open con-
tempt for any important law engenders disrespect for law itself,
so we owe it to our national integrity to make serious attempts at
enforcement. Also, setting aside for the moment the complicated
question of whether newcomers compete with native workers for
jobs, it is indisputable that undocumented immigrants who take
jobs in labor-short occupations deny places to would-be lawful
immigrants who live in nations from which illegal entry is less
practical. It is to these equally desperate and ambitious migrants
that our ineffective border control is most unfair.

When we attempted to rescue respect for law by abandoning
our 55 mph speed limit in rural areas because most people
flouted it, we established a new limit of 65 mph, a level we
thought drivers would respect. But for illegal immigration, there
is no analogous solution, because the most sophisticated analysts
can't make a reasonable guess at the level of immigration that
must be allowed before control is practical. Even today's educated
guess would change tomorrow, based on political developments
abroad (like the Tiananmen massacre or the overthrow of Aris-
tide) or changes in economic growth rates and job creation in
places like Mexico and the Dominican Republic. The reality
would also change with job opportunities here. Fewer immigrants
would come if they knew there was no work awaiting them; even
in poor countries, people rarely want to leave their families and
communities. It's not that the pressure for illegal immigration is
so great that if we relaxed our barriers, we'd be inundated with
hordes of immigrants. Though nobody knows how many Mexicans would actually immigrate if they could do so unimpeded, the
number is smaller than most Americans think. Early in this century, after all, when Mexicans were even poorer relative to Americans than they are today, American railroads and farmers had to
send recruiters to Mexico to beg laborers to come.

In Europe, experts feared there would be massive migration
of poor Italians to high-wage countries like France and Germany
when the European Community (EC) was established, so Italian
emigration was restricted. When restrictions were finally abandoned in 1968, however, few Italians left home. The wage differ-
ential between Germany and Italy was still four to one, but for

most Italians, the income difference wasn't great enough to make the upheaval worthwhile. Today, despite continuing income differences between countries like Ireland, Spain, Greece, and Italy, on the one hand, and France and Germany on the other, only 1.5 percent of the EC's population was born in a different EC country from the one in which they now reside. The EC has lots of immigrants—but most come from poorer countries in Africa, Eastern Europe, and the Middle East.

· Americans who are frustrated with our country's inability to regulate immigration might reflect on the experience of other industrial nations, even those with less inclusive traditions. Japan, for example, with its aging workforce and declining fertility rate, also has a need for low-wage immigrants, even now in a stagnant economy. Since 1989 Japan has crafted a temporary, and racist, solution by recruiting some 200,000 (according to official government figures) South American workers who have partial Japanese ancestry. But professional smuggling rings are already at work importing South Americans with documents faking Japanese bloodlines. As immigration expert Wayne Cornelius points out, of the 30,000 Peruvians now in Japan, half may be illegal. In addition to those counted in official data, there may be as many as 250,000 Brazilians who came to Japan as "tourists" and then stayed on to work. Japan also has illegal immigrants from Malaysia, Thailand, Iran, Bangladesh, and Pakistan who overstayed tourist visas. And there are 700,000 Koreans living in Japan, many descended from laborers imported by force during Japan's prewar occupation of Korea, others who immigrated illegally in recent years. The sociologist Nathan Glazer remarked a few years ago that "one does not note in Japan, a country with very few immigrants, unmade hotel beds, unwashed dishes in restaurants, unmanned filling stations. It seems there is a way of managing even without immigrants." Glazer should look again. In 1992 alone, 280,000 foreigners came to Japan on short-term visas and then disappeared into the country.

And then there is France, whose new conservative government proclaims a goal of "zero immigration." It's a fantasy. There are already one million undocumented immigrants living in France, with another 4.5 million foreigners there legally—mostly Algerians, Moroccans, and Tunisians. All told, immigrants make up over 10 percent of France's population, and many have relatives and friends who are ready to join them, legally or illegally.

Last year, one thousand would-be immigrants drowned while

trying to swim to Spain. Uncounted others made it, ferried to a point two hundred yards from shore by Moroccan smugglers. In return for a promise of $2 billion in aid from the EC, Morocco has now agreed to station 3,500 troops on its beaches to try to deter human smuggling, yet the illegal immigration continues. In Germany there are nearly two million Turkish immigrants, brought into the country over a thirty-year period as "guest workers," who never went home. All told, there are probably five million undocumented immigrants in Western Europe, 1.5 percent of the population. In the United States, there are perhaps three and a half million undocumenteds, a slightly smaller share of our population, though we have another three million formerly undocumented persons who were "legalized" after the 1986 amnesty. Our self-image of America as a nation uniquely open to immigration is historically accurate but less true today. Although our immigration restrictionists are now more civilized than those in Germany, the 8.5 percent of our population that is foreign-born is not much greater than the 8.2 percent of German residents who came from elsewhere. In 1920, however, over 13 percent of Americans were foreign born. *Then* we were unique, not now, when throughout the world, one hundred million people are immigrants in one country or another.

Push and Pull

All industrialized nations have an "immigration problem" for similar reasons. When labor markets are tight or we want agricultural or service work performed cheaply, we welcome immigrants, sometimes without restriction, sometimes through official "guest worker" programs. But bringing guest workers into a country is easier than sending them home. Once they arrive, it is virtually impossible to prevent them from leaving the jobs for which they were recruited and finding other work.

It used to be easier to send immigrants back when their work was done, because their wives were content to wait for them at home. But many Mexican women, for example, are no longer willing to stay home while their husbands travel back and forth to earn money in the United States. Now, women want to come north to work as well, either with their husbands or independently. Since 1987 alone, the number of Mexican women attempting to cross the border illegally has doubled, while the number of men has not changed. A consequence is declining return migration for men.

Once an immigrant group establishes a presence, networks linking immigrants with their home country become difficult to break. In the United States, we give priority for legal immigration to "family reunification," meaning that immigrants can bring their relatives here at the head of the line. For example, workers amnestied under the 1986 law will soon be eligible to bring in family members—several million additional legal residents.

Few immigrants leave home without some idea of how to find work in America. Once an immigrant community is established here, this becomes a lot easier. Immigrants recruit friends and relatives from back home when their employers need additional help. In the garment districts of Los Angeles, New York, or Miami, entire plants are staffed by immigrants from the same small village in Mexico, El Salvador, or China. Once such powerful networks are established, policy is impotent to break them.

When George Bush and Carlos Salinas first began promoting a North American Free Trade Agreement (NAFTA), one of their claims was that providing more jobs in Mexico would reduce the Mexicans' desire to emigrate. The claim is heard less frequently now, because it's become clear that the relationship is more complex. Emigration is expensive (the illegal kind often requires hiring a guide and buying false documents for as much as $2,000), and the poorest Mexicans can't afford it. If Mexico becomes more prosperous, more people will have money to pay for emigration.

Traditional societies send few emigrants, but the disruption of traditional ways spurs emigration. As countries industrialize, formerly rural workers, now more rootless, begin to think of the next step—emigration. Industrial workers aspire to better jobs, and when they reach the limit of their upward mobility at home, think of the next step—emigration. Undocumented Mexican immigrants are almost never those without jobs at home; they have above-average education and aspirations whetted by urban industrial employment. In the 1970s, South Korea's economy was the fastest growing in the world, and its emigration rate to the United States was also the fastest growing.

Today, the ratio of U.S. to Mexican wages is about seven to one, and the ratio of living standards (measured purchasing power) is about three to one. As this gap narrows, economic growth and development in Mexico will initially stimulate *increased* emigration to the United States. At some point in the future, most experts believe, the gap will become small enough that emigration will slow. But nobody can hazard a guess about when that point might come—one U.S. government commission recently concluded it could take "several generations." Something short of full equality with U.S. incomes is necessary. Few Americans, after all, move from city to city in search of relatively small wage increases, so long as they have a job at home. Mexicans are even less likely to abandon their culture and homeland for small income differences. As noted earlier, a four-to-one ratio wasn't enough to spur Italian moves to Germany.

Immigration flows are even more immune to policy influences because the relationship between economic status at home and the propensity to migrate varies from society to society and from time to time. By 1980, one-third of working-age persons born in Puerto Rico had migrated to the mainland. The migrants were Puerto Ricans with below-average education levels, and they were more likely to be unemployed before leaving the island— just the opposite of today's Mexican immigrants. Why? According to economists Alida Castillo-Freeman and Richard Freeman, it's because Congress raised Puerto Rico's minimum wage so high that island unemployment increased; for the remaining jobs, employers were able to select only the most qualified workers, who then chose not to migrate and accepted relatively good pay at home. Those left on the streets migrated. By establishing a high minimum wage for Puerto Rico, Congress in effect determined that it was better to bring unskilled Puerto Rican migrants to New York than to send New York jobs to Puerto Rico. Had the Puerto Rican minimum wage been lower, fewer islanders would have migrated, but more factories would have left the mainland for the island's low wage haven. Can we conclude from the Puerto Rican experience that Mexican migration will slow if Mexican wages are kept low? No: too many other factors will intervene.

In reality, NAFTA and trade policy could become irrelevant to the volume of future immigration flows from Mexico, since, as Wayne Cornelius suggests, these factors are likely to be swamped by Mexico's domestic agriculture policy. Before President Salinas's policies of economic liberalization, Mexico subsidized peasants to remain in rural areas; the government, for example, bought corn from peasants at twice the world price and prohibited the sale of communal farm lands to private investors. But last year the Mexican Constitution was amended to permit these lands to be sold, and it is widely expected that corn and bean subsidies will decline. The purpose of these policies is to encourage investment in efficient cash crops for export, but if successful, they will result in many fewer peasants working the land: approximately one million peasants are expected to leave farming annually during the next ten to twenty years. The Mexican labor force is already growing at the rate of one million jobseekers per year, from three hundred thousand to half a million more than current economic growth can absorb. Emigration pressures will be irresistible, regardless of NAFTA or U.S. border policies.

Paying for Our Pensions

Two claims fuel much of the recent debate about immigration. One is that immigrants draw more on public services (like welfare and public health) than they contribute in taxes. The second is that immigrants take jobs from the rest of us.

It is true that local government is burdened by immigrant services. Over 10 percent of California's immigrants are on welfare, and over 25 percent of southern California's jail population are immigrants. But at the same time, our national budget is becoming more dependent on immigrant taxes. Fewer Americans will be working when the baby boom generation (born between 1946 and 1964) begins to reach retirement age in 2010. By that time, we will have spent the boomers' Social Security contributions to offset the federal budget deficit. So we'll need the taxes of younger working immigrants to pay Medicare and Social Security for the older generation. The services–taxes balance of which we now complain will become a national, not a local issue. And immigrants will become part of the solution, not the problem.

Today, 12 percent of Americans are over sixty-five years old, and their health and retirement benefits consume about one-third of all federal spending. When the baby-boom generation retires, 20 percent will be over sixty-five. No longer paying income or Social Security taxes, they will instead consume Social Security and Medicare. These benefits can be paid for only by large tax increases on those still working, by big jumps in productivity or by changes in the ratio of working to retired Americans.

We can improve the ratio if we make people work longer and raise their retirement age. Minor steps have already been taken: the normal retirement age for Social Security will be raised to sixty-seven in 2027, and further increases are inevitable. We can also improve the ratio with an increase in birth rates, so that more young workers are available to replace those who retire. This is also happening: the fertility rate (children borne by the average

woman) has jumped from 1.87 to 2.05 in the last five years. But
this is not something we necessarily want to encourage; it contradicts, for example, our desire to reduce teen pregnancies.

Ultimately, we can't increase the working-to-retired ratio
enough without a lot more immigration. While only 26 percent of
the U.S. population is now in the prime working age of twenty to
thirty-nine, 46 percent of immigrants are in that age group. Retir-
ing baby boomers need people who contribute more in taxes than
they consume in services. Immigration will have to be an increasing part of the solution, not only in the United States, but
throughout the industrial world. Germans now retire at age sixty,
but the sixty-and-over set, now 21 percent of Germany's population, will make up 30 percent by the year 2020. With fewer workers to pay that many pensions, Germany has increased its retirement age to sixty-five, effective in 2012. Germany needs more
young Turks, not fewer. Japan's fertility rate is only 1.53 and, in
thirteen years, Japan is expected to become the first country in
the world where over 20 percent of the population is older than
sixty-five, a point the United States can expect to reach by 2025,
unless there is a lot more immigration.

Competition for Jobs

Do immigrants take jobs from residents? In some cases they
do and in others they provide labor no native group is willing to
supply. It is impossible to design an immigration policy that bars
the "takers" and welcomes the "providers."

Important industries (garment manufacturing, for example)
could not exist without an immigrant labor supply; no native
workers are available or willing to work in these industries even in
periods of high unemployment. If natives were willing to work,
they would demand wage-and-benefit packages that would certainly make the industries uncompetitive with companies based
abroad. Our minimum wage is now so low, however, that lawful
employers can survive by paying the minimum to immigrant
workers, while sweatshop operators exploit immigrants' vulnerability and collect an additional premium. Because of immigrant seamstresses, an industry exists that supports not only its
professional and managerial employees but a variety of upstream
workers in computer software, machine tools, textiles, and pet-
rochemicals. In Los Angeles, with mostly undocumented immigrant workers, the garment industry has grown in the last decade,

while manufacturing as a whole, and especially garment manufacturing, has declined nationwide.

There is also no displacement of native workers in low-wage
service jobs, in restaurant kitchens, say, or hotels. It is, of course,
theoretically possible that restaurants and hotels could be forced
to pay wages high enough to attract American high-school graduates, but if they did so, we'd have many fewer (because much
more expensive) vacations and conventions, not to mention meals
away from home.

American upper-middle-class life is dependent on immigrant
workers performing tasks at wages no established resident would
consider. Zoe Baird didn't need to hire an illegal immigrant to
care for her child; she could have afforded to pay good wages.
But most two-job families or single parents are not in Baird's
income class. Immigrant wages for housecleaning, lawn mowing,
child care, and even carwashing make work outside the home
feasible for people who could otherwise not afford it. Those who
dream of cities without poorly educated, low-wage immigrants
should be required to describe what middle-class and even lower-
middle-class life would be like without them. It can't be done, but
the fantasy persists that a policy could be devised that welcomes
the restaurant, hotel, and personal service workers on whom we
obviously depend, but bans all others.

Another important industry that could not exist but for immigrants is horticulture. In a way, George Bush's inability to banish
broccoli from health-conscious American diets is one cause of
undocumented immigration. Harvest of corn, wheat, and other
grains is mechanized, but fruit, vegetable, and nut horticulture,
occupying only 1 percent of U.S. farmland, is labor intensive and
consumes 40 percent of total farm wages. A broccoli crop, for
example, requires fifty-two labor-hours per acre. According to
agricultural economists Phil Martin and Edward Taylor, U.S.
acreage devoted to broccoli increased by 50 percent in the 1980s
as Americans' annual fresh broccoli consumption almost tripled
to 4.5 pounds per person. Broccoli alone brought two thousand
migrant farmworkers from rural Mexico to the United States.
Other healthy fruits and vegetables had a similar impact; fresh
tomato consumption jumped from thirteen to eighteen pounds
per person, and U.S. production grew by 38 percent. Production
of all vegetables combined rose by 33 percent, because even imports from countries like Mexico and Chile couldn't satiate Americans' hunger for more vitamins and roughage. Besides, Latin

Americans also want to stay healthy. Carlos Salinas's goal of "exporting tomatoes, not tomato pickers" is frustrated by Mexicans' consumption of tomatoes at twice the per capita rate of Americans. Even rapid expansion of Mexican tomato acreage won't replace U.S. growers' demands for immigrant labor.

Bush did make something of a contribution to solving the problem. Since fresh vegetable consumption rises with upscale lifestyles, holding down personal income growth kept vegetable acreage from increasing even more than it did. Martin and Taylor report that fresh vegetables have high "elasticities"; in other words, a 1 percent increase in family income is associated with a 1 percent increase in broccoli and lettuce consumption and a 2.4 percent increase for cauliflower. So if the Clinton administration succeeds in reversing the trend of declining family income, Americans will eat even more veggies, requiring more rural immigrants, legal or not.

Factoring these kinds of variables into rational immigration rules is beyond the ability of any policy maker. We can let migrant workers in as the demand for vegetables expands, but how do we reduce the number of "guests" when demand contracts, and how can we require them to avoid enticing their brothers and cousins to join them? Communist governments were mostly successful at preventing workers from being employed without authorization, but no other governments have been able to do so.

There are also industries where immigrants do compete with natives, and this competition not only creates native unemployment but reduces wages for those who remain at work as well. Here's one example: fifteen years ago, residential drywallers—the people who erect plasterboard for interior home walls—were represented by the carpenters union in southern California. They averaged about $1,100 in weekly earnings, in today's dollars. Union drywall agreements required homebuilders to pay for full family health insurance. Each employer contributed to a vacation and pension fund for each hour worked. But in the late 1970s, contractors began to hire Mexican immigrants to work without union contract protection. Immigrant workers in turn recruited their friends and relatives, and by 1982 enough nonunion drywallers (many from just one town in rural Mexico) were available, and the contractors stopped hiring union labor altogether. With the carpenters union out of the picture, contractors also dropped their health insurance plans, stopped paying into vacation and pension funds, and cut wages. Contractors now dealt only with labor brokers who paid workers in cash and ignored income-tax withholding, Social Security, unemployment insurance, and minimum-wage laws. By 1992, drywallers worked nearly sixty hours a week to take home $300 in cash, with no benefits. In an atypical action, these undocumented immigrant construction workers went on strike to bring back the carpenters union. A clever union lawyer went after the contractors for minimum-wage violations and used the potential back-pay liability to leverage a strike settlement that included reinstatement of health insurance and a wage increase. Drywallers now earn about double what they got before the strike, and about half what nonimmigrant workers earned a decade earlier.

The construction industry where immigrants displaced native workers and the vegetable industry where no natives choose to work are extreme ends on a scale of displacement. Advocates of loosening border controls cite the former; advocates of tightening cite the latter. Some industries, like garment, can be cited by each. Fifteen years ago, undocumented immigrants fully displaced African-American garment workers in many cities, because the immigrants were willing to tolerate wages and conditions far below what legal workers were used to. In Los Angeles, for example, fifty-five thousand native garment workers were displaced by immigrants in the 1970s. But today, international competition in garment assembly has become so fierce that a domestic industry probably could not survive if it paid the wages of fifteen years ago. Can immigrants, therefore, be said to have displaced African-American workers in the garment industry? Yes and no.

It's probably the case that today, more immigrants are working in jobs natives don't want than in competitive occupations. But even though laid-off aerospace engineers don't normally seek work as gardeners or carwashers, this is a hard argument to make when unemployment is high and wages are declining. And the argument will become even harder if the proposals of some reformers—to increase the immigration of skilled workers—become law. Expanding legal immigration quotas for professional and technical workers will certainly increase competition for scarce jobs.

Solutions

Total border control is an unrealizable dream; it is impossible to calculate immigration flows to match domestic employment needs; and a variety of uncontrollable and unpredictable economic, political, and social developments in sending countries will, in any event, have a lot to do with the actual level of immigration. As candidate Clinton realized, we can't hope to design a coherent immigration policy. But there are piecemeal policies we can implement that address some of the problems, at least around the edges.

These reforms might, if we are lucky, combine with other political and economic developments to slow the "push" of immigrants from sending countries, provide some additional protection for native workers in those few industries where competition with immigrants is a reality, and encourage more honorable and responsible treatment of immigrants, who, in any event, will continue to arrive. It's not that stepped-up border patrols are entirely useless; it's just that we shouldn't delude ourselves into believing that massive national and international political and economic forces can be reversed by more vigilant policing.

One important reform would be a Mexican development program that goes beyond free trade. If we truly want less Mexican immigration, persuading the Mexican government to slow its agricultural liberalization would be one approach. Failing that, we could underwrite a targeted industrial policy in Mexico, which, in violation of free trade rules, would subsidize the development of small industries in rural areas were peasants are being displaced. Funds spent in this way might be more effective than hiring more border patrol agents.

Similarly, a more aggressive and earlier defense of Haiti's democratic government was, in retrospect, the only sensible (and morally decent) immigration policy we could have adopted with regard to that country's boat people. The civil wars in Central America and Indochina, whatever else they might have been, will ultimately have affected America most by raising immigration flows—as any tour through Salvadoran, Vietnamese, and Cambodian communities in California will attest. But these likely results are rarely considered when foreign policy is fashioned.

Better labor standards enforcement in this country would also address parts of the problem. If labor law had been reformed so it wasn't so easy for construction contractors to abandon their contractual relationships with trade unions, it might have been more difficult for immigrants to displace union members in California's homebuilding industry. Enforcement of minimum wage, health and safety, and other workplace rules could reduce, albeit only marginally, incentives for employers to substitute immigrants for natives in other industries where real competition takes place.

Higher labor standards in immigrant industries where native workers don't choose to work would also ameliorate political conflict over the unavoidable presence of undocumented workers. A national health insurance plan, for example, that covered all workers whether here legally or not, would relieve the burden of taxpayers to provide for immigrant health in public emergency rooms and hospitals. Minimum-wage enforcement in immigrant industries, along with a more hospitable climate for union organizing, would put more money into immigrant neighborhoods and increase their tax contributions to the broader community, while reducing immigrant use of welfare, food stamp, and similar benefits.

And also, of course, we could stop eating broccoli.

CAMPAIGN ADDRESS[3]

It is good to be back home again. As you know, Shelley and I spent ten wonderful weeks here in the winter of 1992, and we will never forget your generosity and your support when we came up here to New Hampshire, and you and I stood together to say to the national establishment of both parties, "Turn around. You're going the wrong way!"

We may have lost that nomination, my friends, but you and I have won the battle for the heart and soul of the Republican Party.

Four years ago, we came here to say no to tax hikes and no to quota bills, and now every Republican says no to tax hikes and no to quota bills and no to affirmative action.

So, we want first to welcome the prodigal sons home to their father's house.

But we shall remind them: The Buchanan Brigades are not leap-year conservatives. We have borne the day's heat. We have

[3]Speech delivered by Patrick J. Buchanan, syndicated columnist and presidential aspirant, at the Manchester Institute of Arts and Sciences in Manchester, New Hampshire on March 20, 1995, from *Vital Speeches of the Day* 61:461–63 My 15 '95. Copyright © 1995 by *Vital Speeches of the Day*. Reprinted with permission.

labored in these vineyards from the very first hour. And we stand here today to resume command of the revolution that we began here three years ago—because we intend to lead that revolution to triumph and into the White House in 1996.

But this campaign is not about yesterday. It is about tomorrow. It is about America's future. It is about taking America forward toward the dream of a Constitutional Republic that first stirred in the hearts of the boys who stood their ground on the Lexington Green and the men who held at the Concord Bridge. This campaign is about an America that once again looks out for our own people and our own country first.

Three years ago when I came to New Hampshire, I went up to the North Country on one of my first visits. I went up to the James River paper mill. It was a bad day, just before Christmas, and many of the workers at the plant had just been laid off. They were sullen and they were angry and they didn't want to talk to anyone.

So as I walked down that line of workers, I will never forget: Men shook my hand and looked away. Then one of them, with his head down, finally looked up, and with tears in his eyes said, "Save our jobs." As I rode back down to Manchester, I wondered what it was I could do for that factory worker.

When I got back to Manchester that night, I read a story in the Union Leader about the U.S. Export-Import bank funding a new paper mill in Mexico.

What are we doing to our own people? What is an economy for if not so that workers and their families can enjoy the good life their parents knew, so that incomes rise with every year of hard work, and so that Americans once again enjoy the highest standard of living in the world? Isn't that what an economy is for?

Our American workers are the most productive in the world; our technology is the finest. Yet, the real incomes of American workers have fallen 20 percent in twenty years.

Why are our people not realizing the fruits of their labor?

I will tell you. Because we have a government that is frozen in the ice of its own indifference, a government that does not listen anymore to the forgotten men and women who work in the forges and factories and plants and businesses of this country.

We have, instead, a government that is too busy taking the phone calls from lobbyists for foreign countries and the corporate contributors of the Fortune 500.

Well, I have not forgotten that man at James River, and I have come back to give him my answer here in New Hampshire.

When I am elected president of the United States, there will be no more NAFTA sellouts of American workers. There will be no more GATT deals done for the benefit of Wall Street bankers. And there will be no more $50 billion bailouts of Third World socialists, whether in Moscow or Mexico City.

In a Buchanan White House, foreign lobbyists and corporate contributors will not sit at the head of the table. I will.

We're going to bring the jobs home and we're going to keep America's jobs here, and when I walk into the Oval Office, we start looking out for America first.

So, to those factory workers in the North Country and to the small businessmen and businesswomen, I say to you: This campaign is about you. We are on your side.

Whatever happened to the idea of Americans as one nation, one people? Whatever happened to the good, old idea that all Americans, of all races, colors and creeds, were men and women to whom we owed loyalty, allegiance and love? What happened to the idea that America was a family going forward together?

When I was writing my column a couple of months ago, I read a story from New York about fifty-eight new partners made at Goldman Sachs, each of whom had gotten a bonus of at least $5 million that year. Fine. One month later, the story ran that because profits were down at Goldman Sachs, 1,000 clerical workers were being laid off—1,000 men and women at the lowest levels at Goldman Sachs. That was a shameful act of corporate greed.

But let me tell you about another story. Down in LaGrange, Georgia, I visited one of the most modern textile plants in America—only this textile plant had been burned to the ground. All the employees were saved, but the factory was a total ruin. And, after the fire, when the factory workers were called into the assembly hall of the administration building, they thought they were going to be told what so many others have been told before: Now that the plant has burned, we'll be moving to Mexico or Taiwan.

But the managers of the Milliken plant came down from Spartanburg and they said to these 600 workers: You are our family. We have suffered a loss together. We are going to look for a new job for every single worker in this plant, and beyond that, we're going to build a brand new Milliken plant, the most modern in the world, right here on this site in LaGrange, Georgia. We want our workers to join together and help us build it.

And in August it will rise again. And every one of those workers will be kept on and brought back to his old job.

Isn't that the idea of free enterprise we Republicans and conservatives believe in? Isn't that the idea and the spirit of one people working together that we must recapture? So I say to the workers and managers at that textile plant down in LaGrange, Georgia, and to all the other plants and businesses and small businesses around America: This campaign is about you. This fight is your fight.

And we Americans must also start recapturing our lost national sovereignty.

The men who stood at Lexington and at Concord Bridge, at Bunker Hill and Saratoga, they gave all they had, that the land they loved might be a free, independent, sovereign nation.

Yet, today, our birthright of sovereignty, purchased with the blood of patriots, is being traded away for foreign money, handed over to faceless foreign bureaucrats at places like the IMF, the World Bank, the World Trade Organization and the U.N.

Look how far we have gone:

A year ago, two United States helicopters flying surveillance over northern Iraq were shot down by American fighter planes in a terrible incident of friendly fire. Captain Patrick McKenna of the Citadel, where I just visited, commanded one of those helicopters. Every American on board was killed. And when the story hit the news, the vice president, then visiting in Marrakesh at the World Trade Organization meeting, issued a statement that said the parents of these young men and women can be proud their sons and daughters died in the service of the United Nations.

But those young men and women didn't take an oath to the United Nations. They took an oath to defend the Constitution and the country we love. And let me say to you, when Pat Buchanan gets into that Oval Office as Commander in Chief, no young men and women will ever be sent into battle except under American officers and to fight under the American flag.

So let me say to those brave young patriots who have volunteered to serve in the Armed Forces of the United States to defend us, our peace and our security: This campaign is about you.

Look how far we have gone:

Rogue nations that despise America, right now are plotting to build weapons of mass destruction and to buy or to build the missiles to deliver them to our country. Yet the United States of America remains naked to a missile attack. We have no defense. Why? Because a twenty-year-old compact with a cheating Soviet regime, that has been dead half a decade, prevents us from building our missile defense.

Well, that dereliction of duty ends the day I take the oath.

I will maintain a military for the United States that is first on the land, first on the seas, first in the air, first in space—and I will not ask any nation's permission before I build a missile defense for the United States of America.

To those Americans who have served this country in her wars from Europe to the Pacific, from Korea to Vietnam: This campaign is about you. It is about never letting America's guard down again.

What is the matter with our leaders?

Every year millions of undocumented aliens break our laws, cross our borders, and demand social benefits paid for with the tax dollars of American citizens. California is being bankrupted. Texas, Florida and Arizona are begging Washington to do its duty and defend the states as the Constitution requires.

When I was in California in 1992, I spoke on this issue in San Diego. A woman came, uninvited, to the sheriff's office where I was holding a press conference, and asked if she could join me at that press conference. I said, "Why?" She said, "I had a boy, a teenage boy, who was killed in an automobile accident by drunken drivers who were on a spree, who had walked into this country, had no driver's license and did not belong here."

Three months ago I talked, in the same city of San Diego, to a young Border Patrol agent. He had been decorated as a hero. He showed me the back of his head. There was a scar all over it. Illegal aliens had crossed the border, he went to apprehend them, and they waited to trap him. When he walked into their trap, they smashed his head with a rock and came to kill him. Only when he took out his gun and fired in self defense did his friends come and save his life.

Yet our leaders, timid and fearful of being called names, do nothing. Well, they have not invented the name I have not been called. So, the Custodians of Political Correctness do not frighten me. And I will do what is necessary to defend the borders of my country even it is means putting the National Guard all along our southern frontier.

So, to the people of California, Florida, Texas and Arizona being bankrupted paying the cost of Washington's dereliction of duty, to that brave Border Patrol agent and the men and women who serve with him, and to that woman who lost her boy because her government would not do its duty: This campaign is about you.

And as we defend our country from threats from abroad, we shall fight and win the cultural war for the soul of America.

Because that struggle is about who we are, what we believe, and the kind of people we shall become. And that struggle is being waged every day in every town and school room of America.

When many of us were young, public schools and Catholic schools, Christian schools and Jewish schools, instructed children in their religious heritage and Judeo-Christian values, in what was right and what was wrong. We were taught about the greatness and goodness of this land we call God's country, in which we are all so fortunate to live.

When I was a little boy, three years old, three-and-a-half-years old, my mother's four brothers, one by one, came down to our house, and said good-bye, and we took them to the bus station or the train station to send them off to Europe. Then we got reports from places like Anzio and Sicily, and, in the end, they all came home. But in our school days, when I was five years old or six years old, in first grade, occasionally we would go out in the playground and there would be a short ceremony for some fellow who did not come back from the Ardennes or Anzio or the Bulge.

And that's what we were taught, and that's what we loved.

But today, in too many of our schools our children are being robbed of their innocence. Their minds are being poisoned against their Judeo-Christian heritage, against America's heroes and against American history, against the values of faith and family and country.

Eternal truths that do not change from the Old and New Testament have been expelled from our public schools, and our children are being indoctrinated in moral relativism, and the propaganda of an anti-Western ideology.

Parents everywhere are fighting for their children. And to the mothers and fathers waging those battles, let me say: This campaign is your campaign. Your fight is our fight. You have my solemn word: I will shut down the U.S. Department of Education, and parental right will prevail in our public schools again.

"What does it profit a man if he gain the whole world and suffer the loss of his immortal soul?" That is true also of nations. No matter how rich and prosperous we may become in material things, we cannot lose this battle for the heart and soul of America.

For as de Tocqueville said long ago,

"America is a great country because she is a good country, and if she ceased to be good, she will cease to be great."

Yet, today, America's culture—movies, television, magazines, music—is polluted with lewdness and violence. Museums and art galleries welcome exhibits that mock our patriotism and our faith. Old institutions and symbols of an heroic, if tragic past—from Columbus Day to the Citadel at South Carolina, which graduated Captain McKenna, from Christmas carols in public schools to Southern war memorials—they are all under assault. This campaign to malign America's heroes and defile America's past has as its end: To turn America's children against what their parents believe and what they love.

But because our children are our future, we can't let that happen. We can't walk away from this battle. I pledge to you: I will use the bully pulpit of the Presidency of the United States, to the full extent of my power and ability, to defend American traditions and the values of faith, family, and country, from any and all directions. And, together, we will chase the purveyors of sex and violence back beneath the rocks whence they came.

So, to those who want to make our country America the beautiful again, and I mean beautiful in every way—This campaign is about you.

In the history of nations, we Americans are the freedom party. We are the first people, the only nation dedicated to the proposition that all men and women are created equal, that they are endowed by their creator with the inalienable right to life, liberty, and the pursuit of happiness. And nothing can stop us from going forward to a new era of greatness, in a new century about to begin, if we only go forward together, as one people, one nation, under God.

So to these ends, and for these purposes, I humbly, but proudly, declare my candidacy for the Presidency of the United States.

A POTENT TRINITY—GOD, COUNTRY & ME[4]

Another day on the angry airwaves of America: In a radio studio in a Washington suburb, irate callers popped off about the

[4]Article by David Corn, correspondent for *The Nation*, Washington, D.C. bureau, from *The Nation* 260:913–16 Je 26 '95. Copyright © 1994 by The Nation Company, L.P. Reprinted with permission.

dire threats posed by immigrants, liberals, the Council on Foreign Relations and those damn federal bureaucrats. An enraged fellow from the West exploded; this government, he shouted, is "anti-gun and anti-Christian." The Feds, he ranted, intend to confiscate the guns of God-fearing citizens so that they then can force people into a secular slavery. No one is looking out for *us*, he moaned. As a co-host of this syndicated radio show, I tried to respond with a touch of humor: "Perhaps you need to start the Guns and Christians Party." "That's a good idea!" he exclaimed. The other host chimed in: "Why don't we just call it the Constitution Party." "That would work, too," the caller said. But he fancied my suggestion more. A commercial break loomed. The upset Christian gun aficionado was cut off, the "On Air" sign went dark and the man in the chair next to me laughed deeply. "He's one of mine," a beaming Patrick Buchanan said. "One of mine."

He sure is. Without fully endorsing the caller's paranoid, religious, nationalist schema, Buchanan had spoken to him as a compatriot. This is what Buchanan does dozens of times a day—and has been doing for decades. He delivers a clear message to the most disaffected of the far right: I understand, my friend, and *we* can do something about the onslaught being waged against us by *them*. Over the years Buchanan has fired off overheated blasts against immigrants, welfare recipients, homosexuals, affirmative action beneficiaries, pro-choice advocates and all the other bothersome folks who were not around in what he calls "the America where we grew up." That kind of talk has endeared him to conservatives nationwide. But it is his talent for bonding with the politically far-out without embracing all their looniness that offers him a chance to snatch the prize he currently seeks—the Republican presidential nomination. During his radio show (which he abandoned in March, along with his syndicated newspaper column and CNN gig as *Crossfire*'s right-hand man, to run for the highest office), he regularly condemned people who act violently against abortion clinics but sympathetically noted that he too feels in his soul the justifiable frustration of those who consider abortion to be mass murder. He refused to pronounce California's Proposition 187 sound public policy, but remarked that it is a valid message being conveyed by set-upon citizens fed up with illegal immigration. Buchanan knows how to connect to the most furious on the right.

Buchanan displayed his narrowcasting skills during a recent twenty-hour trot through New Hampshire. The first stop was the basement of Murphy's Steakhouse in downtown Concord. As twenty Buchananeers waited for the chief to arrive, a few explained why they are backing the talking head: He has never caused them to doubt his loyalty to rock-hard conservatism. Buchanan supporters in New Hampshire sneer at anyone who dares attach the label "conservative" to Bob Dole or Phil Gramm. In the language of this tribe, these candidates are "rhinos" (Republicans in name only). Don't you know, the stalwarts ask, that Dole is a sellout insider, ever eager to compromise away principle? That Gramm is a phony as well? Both encouraged President George Bush to flush his no-new-taxes pledge. Both voted for civil rights legislation. Before recently seeing the light, Gramm had told social conservatives to get lost. Gramm's credentials as a conservative might (in the eyes of this crew) be salvageable, but he bears another severe debit: He has flirted with G.O.P. activists in other states seeking to schedule early primaries and compete with New Hampshire.

But when asked to cite what issue most moves them about Buchanan, a number of those waiting in Murphy's referred to the economic nationalism of his crusades against NAFTA and GATT. Buchanan has howled about trade pacts that benefit transnational corporations at the expense of American workers and surrender U.S. sovereignty to a not-to-be-trusted international establishment, thus melding populism of the left and right. Speaking softly in the accent of his native Germany, Ortwin Krueger, an executive at a local manufacturing concern and a naturalized citizen, explained that eleven years ago he was a Gary Hart man; now he frets that decent industrial jobs are vanishing from his adopted land. And Buchanan is the only candidate who gives a damn.

It was in New Hampshire that Buchanan's economic populism first stirred. When he campaigned in the state in 1992, he encountered people socked by recession. Buchanan had been propelled into that race by his far-right disgust at President Bush's decision to sign a civil rights measure and to renege on the read-my-lips declaration. But while trudging through the Granite State, Buchanan discovered economic dislocation—hard-working Americans hurled out of well-paying jobs. The fault, he concluded, lay with globalization and U.S. trade policy. Since then he has assailed the big banks and corporations that seek these jobs-exporting trade agreements and that finance a slew of lobbyists who guarantee that the trade deals slide through Congress. He is the only Republican contender to acknowledge and address the decline in real wages that has hit middle-income America. In doing so, Buchanan adds fresh troops to the social conservatives in his "Buchanan Brigades." Mad at the Japanese? Outraged your child can't pray in school? Buchanan is out there welding constituencies. Alone in the G.O.P., he attacks Washington as both the Establishment that promotes a liberal secular order *and* the Establishment that pushes the corporatist New World Order. Though also a fierce Catholic foot soldier in service to a conservative social and religious Establishment, Buchanan is the closest thing to a genuine populist in the 1996 race so far.

On this, Buchanan's fourth trip to New Hampshire in seven weeks, his cry was, to hell with federal bureaucrats. (This is the *de rigueur* and easiest portion of the populist script.) The latest federal sin is Goals 2000. It is hardly a blip on the national radar screen, but Buchanan has good reason for fixing on it. New Hampshire is one of a few states that has not accepted funds from this Education Department program. The state was entitled to $2.7 million in Goals 2000 funds, but conservatives in Live Free or Die–land have claimed the program is loaded with weighty federal mandates and pushes a liberal and abortion-rights agenda. A series of front-page articles in the *Concord Monitor* reported that the money arrives virtually free of federal requirements. Nevertheless, the right-wingers were suspicious. So was Buchanan.

In front of local press, Buchanan assailed Goals 2000. It is absurd for Washington to suggest it knows best how to teach children, he snarled, adding that the matter "is somewhat darker than this." The bureaucrats, according to Buchanan, aim to inculcate children with an "animus against American institutions and America's past." Why would this be? Many education professionals, Buchanan explained, "came out of the 1960s" with these attitudes, which are "prevalent in the elite." What are the burdensome regulations of Goals 2000? reporters inquired. Buchanan could not give current examples. Well, then, they asked, how could Goals 2000, which originated in Republican administrations, be a brainwashing program? Ah, Buchanan replied, Goals 2000 is only the beginning: "It is a snake that should be strangled in its crib." To thwart the designs of the anti-American education bureaucrats—a preferred target of the social conservatives— Buchanan wants to defund Goals 2000 and to abolish the Education Department. As he moved from the podium at Murphy's, one excited fan cornered Shelley Buchanan, the candidate's demure-in-public wife, and said in a hushed tone, "Education is a socialistic entity." Shelley smiled at the woman and nodded.

To Buchanan, there is always a larger, "darker" matter. Goals 2000 is another front in the *Kulturkampf* he hailed at the 1992 G.O.P. convention in Houston. (He is utterly unashamed of that performance; his current campaign gladly disseminates copies of the truculent speech, in which he proclaimed himself a crusader in a "religious war . . . for the soul of America.") But Goals 2000 is a battle familiar mostly to the combatants of the right. (Goals 2000 alarms members of New Hampshire's militia movement, who maintain that teachers are deliberately "dumbing down" children to weaken their resistance to socialist indoctrination.) With this broadside, Buchanan reaches the most devout of rightists. At the time of the press conference, neither Dole nor Gramm had muttered a peep on the minicontroversy.

Dole and Gramm know how to pander to the far right. They pay tribute to Ralph Reed and the Christian Coalition by talking the talk. But they cannot compete with Buchanan on the field of ideological purity. During this swing through New Hampshire, Buchanan refused to criticize the local militia movement or the N.R.A. He called for a "Buchanan Security Fence" to be constructed on the U.S.-Mexico border and for a moratorium on *legal* immigration in order to permit the nation "to assimilate and Americanize the citizens already here." He proposed judicial term limits, severe tax cuts and an end to "the cultural pollution poisoning the hearts and minds of our children." He criticized Dole for having opposed an attempt Buchanan made in the Reagan years to kill all federal affirmative action. He decried the "homosexual agenda" (though he said he would not ban gays and lesbians from the White House staff). He urged school prayer and the teaching of creationism ("the truth") in schools. And with his attack on Goals 2000, Buchanan once again proved he walks the walk.

Buchanan, 56, was bred an ideologue in a working-class Washington household where the family icons were Senator Joseph McCarthy, Gen. Douglas MacArthur and Spanish dictator Francisco Franco. (Later on, Buchanan added Chile's tyrant Gen. Augusto Pinochet to his roster of heroes.) His father instilled in him a profoundly conservative Catholic dogma that places its adherents in combat with nonbelievers. As a speech-writer in the Nixon White House, Buchanan was more a guerrilla in the war of ideas than a dirty trickster. During one Florida vacation he holed up with reading material on left-of-center public policy outfits. He returned with a plan to create a conservative policy center and to use the I.R.S. to neutralize these ideological foes. Buchanan's agitation, in part, led to the formation of a secretive I.R.S. unit that collected intelligence on thousands of dissident individuals and organizations and requested audits in hundreds of cases.

After Nixon fell, Buchanan entered the world of high-wire punditry, pounding out syndicated columns and growling on radio and television. He delighted in savage language. For example, he referred to AIDS as nature's "retribution" against homosexuals—and all but praised it as such. In 1985 he was invited into the Reagan White House to supply backbone to an Administration beset by second-term blahs. After that stint, he reclaimed his place in the media firmament. By 1992, Buchanan, the would-be populist, was pulling in close to a million dollars a year.

The quality that makes him a masterful pundit is precisely what hinders his political endeavors: his stridency. He is an advocate who comes on too strong even for some rightists. "Conservatives are principled but should not be nasty," Randall Hekman Jr. of the Michigan Family Forum recently told *Policy Review*. Yet Buchanan is no brooding monster. Media consumers might find it hard to believe that this pit bull is, in person, self-deprecating, good-humored and even charming. In Washington's media circles, he deploys these traits to blunt the impact of his caustic and bellicose bombast. During one radio show earlier this year, when his liberal co-host mentioned Senator Jesse Helms's support for right-wing tyrants in Latin America, a riled-up Buchanan shouted, "You just wait, you just wait," before a commercial break prematurely ended the discussion. He then exploded in laughter. With a red face, he happily explained that he nearly had said on air, "You just wait until 1996, then you'll see a real right-wing tyrant."

There is the nasty business of his alleged anti-Semitism—a subject well raked over in past years. When recently queried on this by a potential supporter in New Hampshire, Buchanan dismissed the charge as a hysterical response to his defense of accused Nazi war criminal John Demjanjuk (who ultimately was cleared of the charge that he was the infamous Nazi guard Ivan the Terrible). But over the years Buchanan has produced an assortment of ugly statements on Holocaust-related topics and the role of Jews in American foreign policy. So much so that William F. Buckley concluded in a 1991 article that Buchanan could not be defended from the allegations of anti-Semitism. In recent years, Buchanan has stayed clear of trouble in this area. But he still exhibits a mean-spirited desire to bash—calculatingly—whole groups of people. Recently in assailing affirmative action, Buchanan asked, "How, then, can the feds justify favoring sons of Hispanics over sons of white Americans who fought in World War II or Vietnam?" Plenty of Hispanic Americans fought in Vietnam, but such a fact did not impede Buchanan, who practices identity politics with unrestrained zeal.

Does this pundit who never held elected office really think he can become President? Buchanan has a plan. Someone has to emerge from the pack as the challenger to Dole, Buchanan figures, and that candidate will likely be a conservative. (Ralph Reed boasts that 42 percent of Republican primary voters are aligned with the religious right.) The contenders for this spot now are Buchanan and Gramm, and Buchanan routinely declares: "I am the one authentic conservative in the race." The goal, then, is for him to place second in Iowa or New Hampshire. Next, the campaigns head toward the South. In South Carolina Buchanan is well positioned, a result of his anti-NAFTA crusade, which was fondly received in this textiles-loaded state. And in states where registered Democrats can vote in Republican primaries—such as Tennessee and Georgia—Buchanan will push his America First platform in a bid for the sort of voters once dubbed Reagan Democrats.

He acknowledges the race may not break his way, but he certainly is in it to attain the nomination, not a Cabinet appointment or higher speaker fees. There actually are reasons for Buchanan to hope. G.O.P. state chairs in Iowa and South Carolina laud his organization efforts in their states, and New Hampshire is chockfull of right-wingers. Attending Buchanan's press conference at Murphy's was Roy Stewart, who chairs Granite State Taxpayers, Inc., and he was leaning toward Buchanan. ("The U.S. first, the hell with the world," Stewart said.) His outfit claims to represent about 15,000 voters, most of them conservatives. The Christian Coalition has a healthy flock in the state. The archconservative and influential *Manchester Union-Leader* has been sweet on Buchanan and downright hostile to Gramm. Gary Bauer of the Family Research Council, James Dobson of Focus on the Family and Beverly LaHaye of Concerned Women of America—each with devoted followings among conservatives—considered jointly endorsing Buchanan. But then Gramm rushed to the pulpit and no triple endorsement emerged. More recently, Bauer helped concoct Dole's Buchananesque anti-Hollywood screed.

Pat Hynes, a state G.O.P. official, observes that conservative *activists* are enlisting in the Buchanan Brigades, but most conservative *voters* seem willing to give Gramm a chance. The local economy has rebounded since 1992 (when Buchanan won 37 percent of the vote against Bush). But enough economic anxiety exists—people working two jobs to get by, settling for lousy benefits—for Buchanan to find a sizable audience for his America First nationalism.

As for money, Buchanan will not match the cash pull of Dole or Gramm, but he will bank enough to fund a full-fledged organization in the early going. In 1992, he raised $8 million, much of it in direct mail, and collected more than $5 million in federal matching funds. In the first three months of this year, before Buchanan was an official candidate, his mail operation and fundraisers netted nearly $1 million. South Carolina textile manufacturers have been very generous. The corporate heads of King Kullen Groceries and Sherwin-Williams paint are financial backers.

And Buchanan, as he sees it, has recent history on his side. Three years ago, he waged a rebellious campaign against his party leaders and used affirmative action, immigration and taxes as his sharpest spears. Look at the Republican Party today, he notes: "We've won the battle for the heart and soul." In the latest poll of G.O.P. voters in New Hampshire he secured that much-sought-after second-place spot, attracting 13 percent behind Dole's 44 percent. Gramm drew a measly 7 percent.

Buchanan may be able to gain the nomination by appealing to both wrathful social conservatives and resentful working-class Americans. Taking the White House is another matter. He is the G.O.P. candidate least capable, temperamentally, of tacking toward the center should he collect the nomination. He comes ready-made to be demonized. Despite his success in rousing conservative activists, playing to voters' enmity toward immigration and affirmative action, and exploiting the populist urges of disaffected blue-collar Americans, Buchanan cannot escape the widespread perception that he is a self-righteous, bullying, vengeful gladiator who yearns too much for a throne of his own. He probably is too true to himself and his convictions to alter this image. That may be the price Buchanan pays for being the truest of believers. A California survey of Republicans found that his negative rating was 32 percent, second in the G.O.P. field to home-grown Governor Pete Wilson.

Buchanan has been rewarded with wealth and prominence for having ferociously fought political struggles he views as nothing less than spiritual warfare. Yet it is not only his delight and dexterity in prosecuting a holy war that is scary, it is his attitude toward democracy itself. Consider his disdainful comments on the "worship of democracy": "Like all idolatries, democratism substitutes a false god for the real, a love of process for a love of country." Such a statement prompts wonder: Could Buchanan's face, with its twinkling eyes and stern jaw, be the visage of American fascism? How far is this patriot willing to go in devotion to his notions of God and country? To the lengths of a Franco or Pinochet? Recall the statement Buchanan made in 1974 as Nixon was in his final descent: "If we have to drift into demagoguery, so be it—we owe them a few." Buchanan's politics are often about payback.

During an appearance in May on a New Hampshire cable show, Buchanan was asked what he thought of a Democratic fundraising letter that tagged Newt Gingrich the "most frightening politician of modern times." Buchanan heaved his body back in his chair, let loose a hearty guffaw—this is a person who enjoys laughing—and replied with a smile, "I thought *I* was."

CLOSETS FULL OF BONES[5]

> *Our own ancestors*
> *Are hungry ghosts*
> *Closets so full of bones*
> *They won't close.*
> —Tracy Chapman

A specter is haunting the west: immigration. From the passage of Proposition 187 in California to the growing anti-immigrant movements in Europe, there is a widespread attempt by economically advanced societies to seal themselves off from the less fortunate. The imagery used to describe these immigrants is

[5]Article by Peter A. Quinn, novelist, from *America* 72:10–13 F 18 '95. Copyright © 1995 by *America*. Reprinted with permission.

almost always the same: Immigrants are to hordes what sheep are to flocks, or lions to prides. They swarm rather than arrive, their faceless uniformity evoking the insect world and its ceaseless, relentless capacity to reproduce.

There is no better description of the passions and fears that immigration engenders than the hysterical vision of approaching apocalypse contained in Jean Raspail's novel, *The Camp of the Saints*. First published in 1973, *The Camp of the Saints* tells what happens when a million diseased, crippled, impoverished inhabitants of the Indian subcontinent board a ragtag armada of decrepit ships and descend on the south of France. In Raspail's story, a weak and effete France, awash in liberal guilt and gushing Christian sentimentalism, finds it doesn't have the power to resist.

Neglected for decades, Raspail's book has recently received much attention in Europe and was the subject of a cover article ("Must It Be the Rest Against the West") in the December 1994 issue of *The Atlantic Monthly*. Co-authors Matthew Connelly, a graduate student of history at Yale, and Paul Kennedy, the author of *The Rise and Fall of the Great Powers* (1988), offer a qualified endorsement of the Malthusian and Spenglerian fatalism that is at the heart of Raspail's novel: "Readers may well find Raspail's vision uncomfortable and his language vicious and repulsive, but the central message is clear: we are heading into the twenty-first century in a world consisting for the most part of a relatively small number of rich, satiated, demographically stagnant societies and a large number of poverty-stricken, resource-depleted nations whose populations are doubling every twenty-five years or less."

On the face of it, Raspail's notion of a conscience-stricken West being overwhelmed by an army of disheveled immigrants is less discomforting than laughable. The West has shown itself perfectly capable of using sufficient force whenever its vital interests are at stake—or perceived as being so—as it did most recently in the Gulf War. Indeed, for all the handwringing over immigration and the future of the West, there seems little appreciation that for the last 500 years at least it has been the West that has been threatening and battering the rest of the world, colonizing entire continents and waging war to secure the resources it needs. The current virulent reaction against immigrants in France, Austria and Germany—or, for that matter, the U.S.'s recent treatment of Haitian refugees—is hardly a sign of societies suffering from terminal humanitarianism.

The pessimism evinced by Connelly and Kennedy is mitigated somewhat by their call for international cooperation to deal with the underlying causes of the present population crisis. But as with so many descriptions of the threat posed by the third world, the authors' underlying sense of the West's vulnerability before the procreative puissance of the world's nameless poor is far more vivid and forceful than any formulaic list of possible solutions. The threat is from below, from Raspail's "kinky-haired, swarthy-skinned, long-despised phantoms," from the teeming races that Rudyard Kipling once described as "lesser breeds without the law."

In the United States, the question of intelligence as a distinguishing characteristic between greater and lesser breeds has come to center stage with *The Bell Curve* (1994), the best-selling treatise by Charles Murray and the late Richard J. Herrnstein. Unlike *The Camp of the Saints,* this sedate and statistics-laden book is not directly concerned with immigration, and its central thesis—that I.Q. is a function of race—is more subtle and complex than the horrific vision evoked by Raspail.

Despite their differences, however, there are similarities. At the heart of *The Bell Curve* and *The Camp of the Saints,* as well as of Connelly's and Kennedy's article, is a world in which the central divisions are racial and in which, when all is said and done, the white race is endangered. In fairness to Murray and Herrnstein, they credit Asians with higher I.Q.'s than white Americans. Yet here again is found the implicit threat of a Caucasian community being challenged by another race, one that has been traditionally credited with being shrewder and craftier—in its own "inscrutable" way, smarter—than Westerners.

The fear that white civilization is growing steadily weaker and is at risk of being overwhelmed by barbarians from within and without marks a new life for an old and ugly tradition. The most infamous manifestation of that tradition is the Ku Klux Klan and the host of so-called Aryan resistance groups that continue to spring up on the periphery of American political life. But its most powerful and enduring effect was not limited to cross burnings or rabble-rousing assaults against blacks and immigrants. There was a far more respectable, educated version of this tradition that clothed itself in the language of science and not only won a place in the academy, but helped shape our laws on immigration, interracial marriage and compulsory sterilization of the mentally ill and retarded.

The movement derived its authority from the work of an

Englishman, Francis Galton—Darwin's cousin—who in 1883 published his masterwork, *Inquiries into Human Faculty and Its Development*. In it Galton advocated the modification and improvement of human species through selective breeding and coined a name for it as well: eugenics. In Galton's view, which was shared by many of his Victorian contemporaries and buttressed by a wealth of pseudo-scientific skull measuring and brain weighing, the races were totally distinct. Eugenics, he believed, would give "the more suitable races or strains of blood a better chance of prevailing speedily over the less suitable."

At the turn of the 20th century, the United States was ripe for the gospel of eugenics. The country's original immigrants—Anglo-Saxon and Scots-Irish Protestants—were feeling battered and besieged by the waves of newcomers from southern and eastern Europe (i.e., Italians, Slovaks and Ashkenazi Jews) who were judged so immiscible in appearance and conduct that they would undermine the country's character and identity. According to the eugenicists, the racial "germ plasm" of these groups was riddled with hereditary proclivities to feeblemindedness, criminality and pauperism. These suspicions were given scientific justification by studies that purported to trace family behavior across several generations and discern a clear pattern of inherited behavior.

By the eve of World War I, eugenics was taught in many colleges. Its research arm was generously funded by some of America's wealthiest families, including the Harrimans, Rockefellers and Carnegies. Alfred Ploetz, the German apostle of "racial hygiene," hailed the United States as a "bold leader in the realm of eugenics," a leadership that consisted of the widespread ban on interracial marriage and the growing emphasis on compulsory sterilization.

In the wake of the First World War, the eugenicists helped direct the campaign to halt the "degeneration" of the country's racial stock by changing its immigration laws. As framed by Henry Fairfield Osborn, the president of the Museum of Natural History (at that time a center of eugenic fervor), America would either stop the influx from southern and eastern Europe or it would perish: "Apart from the spiritual, moral and political invasion of *alienism* the practical question of day by day competition between the original American and the alien element turns upon the struggle for existence between the Americans and aliens whose actions are controlled by entirely different standards of living and morals."

The eugenicists played an important role in achieving the Immigration Restriction Act of 1924, a victory noted and approved by Adolf Hitler in his book of the same year, *Mein Kampf*. In fact, nine years later, when the Nazis took power in Germany, they would hail U.S. laws on immigration, intermarriage and sterilization as models for their own legislation.

As successful as the eugenicist crusade was, it was not the first time that the United States had experienced a broad and widely supported campaign against the influx of intractable foreigners whose essential alienism—their alleged lack of moral or mental stamina—would, it was believed, eat away the foundations of American democracy and sink the country into a permanent state of pauperism.

The country's first great immigrant trauma (that is, aside from the forced importation of African slaves) began 150 years ago, in 1845, with the failure of the potato crop in Ireland and the onset of a catastrophe that would result in the death of a million Irish from hunger and disease, and force millions to flee. "The volume of Famine emigration," writes historian Kirby Miller, "was astonishing: between 1845 and 1855 almost 1.5 million sailed to the United States. . . . In all, over 2.1 million Irish—about one-fourth of Ireland's pre-Famine population—went overseas; more people left Ireland in just eleven years than during the preceding two and one-half centuries."

The flight of the Famine Irish produced an immigrant experience unlike any other in American history. There was no web of emigration societies or government agencies to encourage or cushion the process of resettlement abroad. In effect, traditional Irish society—the life of the townslands and the rudimentary agriculture that supported the mass of the Irish tenantry—came apart, dissolving into a chaotic rout. Faced with the simple choice of flee or starve, or in many cases left by eviction with no choice at all, the Irish abandoned the land.

From Liverpool to Boston, contemporary observers remarked on the utter destitution of the Irish who poured into their streets, many of them ill and emaciated and, in the words of one eyewitness, "steeped to all appearances in as hopeless barbarism as the aboriginal inhabitants of Australia."

The dislocation that resulted was enormous. Although the memory of what happened has been softened by the romantic haze that obscures much of our true immigrant history, the passage of the Famine Irish was stark and bitter. Their arrival was the major impetus to the growth of the largest third-party movement in American history, the American or Know-Nothing Party, which was predicated on a loathing for Catholics in general and Irish ones in particular. In the popular mind, the Irish became identified with poverty, disease and violence, a connection strengthened by events like the New York City Draft Riots of 1863, the worst urban uprising ever to occur in the United States. The scale of social turmoil that followed the Irish into America's cities would not be seen again for another century, until the massive exodus of African-Americans from the rural south to the urban north.

Today the sense of the Catholic Irish as wholly alien to white, Christian society seems, perhaps, difficult to credit. But in mid-19th-century America the inalterable otherness of the Irish was for many a given. Indeed, the experience of the Famine Irish seems the historical event closest to the visionary nightmare contained in Jean Raspail's novel. Here in flesh rather than fiction was the descent of a swarming horde of the gaunt and desperate poor on the shores of a smug and prosperous West.

Although eugenics was still a generation away, the theory of Irish racial inferiority was already being discussed. In 1860, Charles Kingsley, English clergyman and professor of modern history at Cambridge University, described the peasants he saw during his travels in Ireland in Darwinian terms: "I am daunted by the human chimpanzees I saw along that hundred miles of horrible country . . . to see white chimpanzees is dreadful; if they were black, one would not feel it so much, but their skins, except where tanned by exposure, are as white as ours."

Three years later, in 1863, Charles Loring Brace, the founder of the Children's Aid Society and a prominent figure in the American social reform movement, published a book entitled *Races of the Old World.* Drawing on the claims of Anglo-Saxon racial superiority found in popular historical works such as Sharon Turner's *History of the Anglo-Saxon* and John Kemble's *The Saxon in England,* Brace located the cause of Irish mental deficiency in brain size, a measurement that served for Victorian ethnologists as an iron indication of intelligence: "The Negro skull, though less than the European, is within one inch as large as the Persian and the Armenian. . . . The difference between the average English and Irish skull is nine cubic inches, and only four between the average African and Irish."

As with so many of his contemporaries, Brace was wrong in

his theory of an Irish "race" stigmatized by shared physical and mental deficiencies. This is not to deny the prevalent poverty of the Irish of Brace's era or the real and formidable problems their poverty presented.

The migration of the rural poor was, is and will always be problematic. But the challenges it presents can only be aggravated by doomsday fearmongering that casts the issue in terms of a vast and imminent *Völkerwanderung* in which the wretched of the earth will infest and overrun Western civilization.

Writing in 1866, Charles Wenworth Dilke recorded his journey across America, Africa and much of Asia. A recent university graduate with high political ambitions, Dilke saw the world caught up in the struggle of light and dark. He framed the future in terms of the competition for survival between the "dear races" (Europeans of Teutonic origin) and the "cheap races" (the hordes of Irish, Indians, Chinese, etc.). For Dilke, "the gradual extinction of the inferior races" was not only desirable but would be "a blessing for mankind."

Dilke was a lofty-minded imperialist. Though contemptuous of other cultures and a racial alarmist, he was no proponent of genocide. Yet we know the kind of final solutions these vicious and simplistic scenarios of racial struggle and survival can lend themselves to. Maybe the Victorians did not. We do.

We need to remind ourselves that immigrants are not a single genus. They come in all shapes and sizes. They have immense strengths and talents as well as liabilities. Their potential for enriching and enlivening the societies that receive them is every bit as real as the difficulties their presence can create.

Certainly, those of us who descend from the Famine Irish would seem to have a special responsibility to look past the current evocation of innumerable, anonymous hordes threatening our borders, or the latter-day recycling of theories of ethnic and racial inferiority, and to see in the faces of today's immigrants the image of our ancestors: those hungry ghosts who, though dispossessed and despised, passed on to us their faith and their hope.

III. PROPOSITION 187 IN CALIFORNIA

EDITOR'S INTRODUCTION

The articles in Section Three focus on Proposition 187 in California, which will have farreaching consequences not only in that state but also across the nation. In the opening article, a 1994 address by Pete Wilson, the Governor of California, announces his intention to file a suit against the federal government for "its failure to control our nation's borders." Wilson claims that there are a million illegal residents in the city of Los Angeles alone, and that since 1988 the taxpayers of California have spent more than $10 billion in education, medical, and prison costs for illegal immigrants. Next an article by Elizabeth Kadetsky, writing in *The Nation,* describes the current political scene in California, which is marked by frequent immigrant-bashing. She writes about two conservative organizations—S.O.S. (Save Our State) and FAIR (Federation for American Immigration Reform)—that are campaigning against illegals as being responsible for a wide array of ills afflicting California, from smog and gigantic traffic snarls to an economy still in recession. Both groups pressed for the passage of Proposition 187, which would bar illegal immigrants from receiving welfare, education, or health benefits (except for emergency medical treatment).

The third article, an editorial in *U. S. News & World Report* by Mortimer B. Zuckerman, the magazine's editor-in-chief, not only advocates Proposition 187 but also declares that it should "be just the starting point" in dealing with immigrants. Zuckerman favors scrapping present immigration policies that favor certain nationalities and instead admitting more people on the basis of their education and professional skills. In an article in *Commentary* published after Proposition 187 was passed in November 1994, Linda Chavez, President of the Center for Equal Opportunity, addresses the key issues of race and entitlements. Today, approximately 80 percent of those legally admitted to the U. S. are from Asia and Latin America, groups involving special problems of assimilation into American society. Public schools, Chavez writes, used to work to acculturate immigrant groups, but now see it as their mission to preserve immigrant language and culture. The demand for Spanish-speaking teachers is so great that some districts, from Los Angeles to Chicago, have been importing instructors from Mexico, Spain, and Puerto Rico. Bilingual curricula in the schools have been a hot point of the immigrant controversy, and Chavez herself advocates their abolition in favor of English-immersion programs that would encourage immigrants to assimilate. She also favors imposing time limits on welfare benefits for refugees, stopping illegal immigration at the border, and denying welfare benefits to illegal aliens already here.

The section's final article, by David Firestone writing in the *New York Times*, reveals the after effects of Proposition 187 as they spread across the country. Ideas from Proposition 187 have already been incorporated into the report of the Congressional Task Force on Immigration Reform, a Republican-dominated panel appointed by Speaker Newt Gingrich. Proposals in the report would require public hospitals to report illegal aliens who seek medical treatment, and force public schools to turn away any students whose parents are in the country illegally. New York City mayor Rudolph Giuliani told Firestone in an interview that such restrictions would have "catastrophic social effects" in New York City and other large urban areas putting thousands of children on the street, driving up crime and delinquency, and contributing markedly to an increase in communicable diseases. The article also notes that in March 1995, the House passed a welfare bill that would deny food stamps, medicaid and welfare payments to legal residents who were not yet citizens. [On November 20, 1995, a federal judge in the United States District Court in Los Angeles declared that certain provisions of Proposition 187 that permit the state to bar children who are illegal aliens from attending public schools are unconstitutional.]

SECURING OUR NATION'S BORDERS[1]

I've come here this afternoon to announce that I will file suit this week against the federal government for its failure to control our nation's borders. It's not a decision I come to lightly. I would rather resolve this crisis in the Congress than in the courts. But the repeated failure of Congress to confront its responsibility to control illegal immigration and to prevent the terrible unfairness to state taxpayers and to needy legal residents—has driven us to seek redress for our injuries in the courts.

The federal government's immigration policy is broken and the time to fix it is now.

It's hard to blame people who day after day pour across our borders. They're coming to find a better life for themselves and their families. It's easy to sympathize with them and even admire their gumption. It is those in Washington that we should condemn—those who encourage the illegals to break the law by rewarding them for their illegal entry.

We are a state and a nation of immigrants, proud of our immigrant traditions. Like many of you, I'm the grandchild of immigrants. My grandmother came to this country in steerage from Ireland at age 16. She came for the same reason any immigrant comes—for a better future than she could hope for in the old country. And America benefited from her and millions like her.

But we, as a sovereign nation, have a right and an obligation to determine how and when people come into our country. We are a nation of laws, and people who seek to be a part of this great nation must do so according to the law.

The United States already accepts more legal immigrants into our country than the rest of the world combined—1.8 million in 1991 alone.

We are a generous people. But there is a limit to what we can absorb and illegal immigration is now taxing us past that limit.

Thousands come here illegally every day. In fact, the gaping

[1]Speech delivered by Pete Wilson, Governor of California, at the Los Angeles Town Hall in Los Angeles, California on April 25, 1994, from *Vital Speeches of the Day* 60:534–6 Je 15 '94 Copyright © 1994 by *Vital Speeches of the Day*. Reprinted with permission.

holes in federal policy have made our borders a sieve. President Clinton has used that very word to describe their porous condition.

The results are, in Los Angeles, there's now a community of illegal residents numbering a million people. That's a city the size of San Diego. Alone, it would be the 7th largest city in the nation—half again the population of our nation's capital, Washington, D.C.

Two-thirds of all babies born in Los Angeles public hospitals are born to illegal immigrants.

As we struggle to keep dangerous criminals off our streets, we find that fourteen percent of California's prison population are illegal immigrants—enough to fill eight state prisons to design-capacity.

And through a recession that has caused the loss of one third the revenues previously received by state government, as we have struggled to maintain per pupil spending and to cover fully enrollment growth with classrooms around the state bursting at the seams, we're forced to spend $1.7 billion each year to educate students who are acknowledged to be in the country illegally.

In total, California taxpayers are compelled *by federal law* to spend more than $3 billion to provide services to illegal immigrants—it's approaching 10 percent of our state budget.

To ignore this crisis of illegal immigration—as some would have us do—is not only irresponsible, but makes a mockery of our laws. It is a slap in the face to the tens of thousands who play by the rules and endure the arduous process of legally immigrating to our country.

It's time to restore reason, integrity and fairness to our nation's immigration policy. And we need to do it now. California can't afford to wait.

First, the federal government must secure our border. That's the first step in securing our future. They must devote the manpower and the technology necessary to prevent people from crossing the border in the first place.

Second, the federal government should turn off the magnetic lure that now rewards people who successfully evade the border patrol and cross the border illegally.

And finally, until our representatives in Washington do act, until they secure the border and turn off the magnetic lure, they should pay the full bill for illegal immigration. The states shouldn't be forced to bear the cost for a failed federal policy that gives a free pass to those who breach our borders, then passes the buck to us.

Those who oppose reform invariably cry racism. They want to stifle even any discussion of the issue.

But this debate isn't about race, it's about responsibility and resources. Washington must accept responsibility for this strictly federal issue, and California must be allowed to devote our limited resources to those people who have come to our country through the legal process.

This isn't a partisan issue, or even simply a California issue. Washington's failure to bear responsibility for illegal immigration is forcing states around the nation to bear enormous costs.

And we have finally started to see some recognition of the problem in Washington. Working with our Congressional delegation on the Budget Resolution before Congress, we've secured the strongest Congressional statement yet for full reimbursement. It fully acknowledges federal responsibility for criminal aliens who have committed felonies under state law only because they were permitted to enter the country illegally by virtue of federal failure to control the border.

In the federal crime bill, the House of Representatives added amendments mandating federal incarceration of criminal aliens or reimbursements to states for the cost of their incarceration—but not until 1998! The official rationale for this four year delay in the arrival of the cavalry is that Congress requires the time to find a way to pay. Meanwhile, the states are to continue patiently laying out what is proportionately a far greater share of our budgets for what is acknowledged to be an exclusively federal duty.

On Friday [Apr. 21, 1995], the Clinton Administration took a positive, but inadequate step towards reimbursing states for the costs of keeping alien felons locked up in state prisons. The $350 million authorized by the White House for all states is little more than half what is required according to the Congressional Budget Office estimate, and in fact is less than they owe California alone.

Another amendment to the crime bill authorizes the addition of 6,000 agents to the Border Patrol, but these House authorizations now must pass the Senate to take effect. And even then, they are just *authorizations,* just acknowledgments of the problem. Congress must then take the next step, *appropriation*—which means voting to actually cut a check to pay the costs imposed on the states by federal failure to control the borders and federal mandates to provide services to illegal immigrants.

And we've watched, time and time again, as Congress has authorized reimbursement in the spring, but then stripped out or failed to pass an appropriation, and left us holding the bag in the fall.

That's why we have launched an unprecedented offensive by a bipartisan coalition of seven states, including the five most populous, to pressure the Administration and Congress to do equity and honor the federal obligation to reimburse us. They should do so in the federal budget and appropriation bills.

But, we will not stand by and watch the political process fail once again, when we can wait no longer. So, in addition to pursuing reform in Washington, we are launching a series of lawsuits against the federal government starting this week. Unfortunately, Congress' track record of failure has compelled us to seek a remedy in the courts, even as we continue a bipartisan, multi-state effort to pressure the Administration and Congress to atone for and pay for their sins by corrective action both at the border and in the appropriation process.

In court, we'll seek two broad goals. First, that the federal government enforce our nation's immigration laws and secure our nation's border.

And second, that the federal government reimburse California fully for costs incurred when it fails to enforce the law.

Suing for reimbursement is not only a matter of fairness for state taxpayers, it's a matter of making the political process work for our nation.

Immigration and control of our nation's border are, by virtue of the Constitution, a strictly federal responsibility. But today, there is no fiscal accountability for that policy.

The Congress is writing blank checks on other people's bank accounts—and one of those accounts belongs to the taxpayers of California.

Congress must be forced to bear the fiscal consequences for its immigration policy. If they have to pay the bill for that policy, if they feel the pinch in the federal budget for which they alone are accountable to the voters, then and only then will they have the incentive to fix this policy that simply doesn't work.

President Clinton has acknowledged as much himself. In the summer [of 1993] he said,

"One of the reasons the federal government has not been forced to confront this . . . is that the states of California, Texas and Florida have had to bear a huge portion of the costs for the failure of federal policy."

It's a fundamental element of democracy—a government must be held accountable for its actions.

And if the federal government were held accountable they would quickly discover that the cost of ignoring the real and explosively growing problem of illegal immigration is far greater than the cost of fixing it.

They would see that the federal resources necessary to secure our nation's border are dwarfed by the billions that California and other states spend today in making massive illegal immigration to America a safety-net for the world. What's more, by compelling California to provide this safety-net for illegals, the feds are tearing gaping holes in the safety-net we seek to provide for our own needy legal residents.

For next year, the Clinton Administration proposes increasing spending on border enforcement across the country by just $180 million a year. We'll spend nearly ten times that amount just educating illegal immigrants in California schools.

Last week I went to El Paso, where I saw firsthand a program known as Operation Hold the Line that has used a blockade to reduce illegal crossings by 75 percent.

I will concede that the same plan that has produced such success for the El Paso Blockade can't be precisely reproduced everywhere on that border. But the most important lesson to draw from El Paso is the we *can* control our border.

Those who say the effort is futile . . . those who say we should simply concede that people who want to cross the border will . . . are wrong.

But to secure our border, we first need a plan. Then we must devote the will and resources to carry it out, as they have in El Paso.

But the officials responsible in Washington fail to see the urgency of the problem.

INS Commissioner Doris Meissner, recently said, and I quote, "There's nothing wrong in taking a year or two [to enact immigration reform.]"

Well, Ms. Meissner, I don't know what border you're looking at, but as the people who bear the cost for your failed policy, we can tell you that two years is too long to wait. Every *day* we wait, the problem grows worse.

That's why we're taking our case to court. Since we must, we will force the federal government to bear responsibility for its policies.

Our first lawsuit, to be filed this week, will seek reimbursement for the costs California bears for incarcerating alien felons in our state prisons. The price tag this year alone is nearly $400 million, and that doesn't include the costs from previous years, the capital costs for housing these criminals, or the costs to county governments.

But our suit will also seek to compel the federal government to do its duty to enforce immigration laws already on the books.

Specifically, we'll demand that the federal government be forced to take custody of the thousands of alien felons who have completed their sentences in state prison, but are back on the street, because the INS has failed to deport them. That federal dereliction forces California to supervise parole for 4,400 criminal aliens every day.

We'll demand that the federal government begin prosecuting alien felons who return to the U.S., currently a federal offense punishable by up to fifteen years in prison, but one routinely ignored by federal officials.

And we will demand that federal officials be required to deport alien criminals to the interior of their home country and not continue the absurd practice of simply dumping them at the border, where all too often they simply re-enter the U.S. across the porous border and beat the bus back to L.A.

We'll file additional suits in the weeks ahead to address other parts of the federal government's failed policy—a policy that has cost the taxpayers of California more than $10 billion in education, medical and prison costs for illegal immigrants since 1988.

And I'm encouraging the cities and counties of California to also file suit to seek reimbursement for the costs owed to them by the federal government.

Our goal, though, is larger than simply seeking reimbursement—as important and as urgently needed as it is.

Our goal is to force the federal government to accept responsibility for the crisis of illegal immigration. Only when they accept responsibility will Congress finally adopt the reforms necessary to restore integrity and fairness to our immigration laws.

Once Congress is forced to confront this problem, I'm sure it will waste no time in doing what's necessary to secure our nation's borders.

And securing our nation's borders is the only way we can secure the future we want for California.

Thank you very much.

BASHING ILLEGALS IN CALIFORNIA[2]

Parrish Goodman had just saved a burdened shopper the
trouble of returning her grocery cart and was back at the expanse
of sidewalk outside Ralph's supermarket in West Los Angeles
competing with the whoosh of the electric doors. Goodman
greeted all who passed in such a friendly way that they tended to
thank him for his cryptic, millionth-generation photocopies that
were equal parts longhand and typewriter script. "You'll be voting
on this in November," he'd say, winking, all courtesy and ambi-
guity.

Goodman was campaigning for Proposition 187, the grandi-
osely titled "Save Our State" ballot initiative that, if passed this
November and validated by the courts over the next several years,
will use strict verification requirements to prevent California's
estimated 1.7 million undocumented immigrants from partaking
of every form of public welfare including nonemergency medical
care, prenatal clinics and public schools. The measure would require employees at public health facilities, welfare offices, police
departments and schools to demand proof of legal residency and
to report those who can't produce it to the Immigration and
Naturalization Service; it also calls for stiff penalties for creating
or using false documents. While conceding that the measure actually does nothing to deter immigration at its source—at the border and with the employers who encourage workers to cross it—
advocates say S.O.S. responds to California's economic downturn
by making life so difficult for the undocumented that they will
either go home or never show up to begin with.

The opposition runs the gamut from those who dispute the
premise that immigrants contribute to hard times to those who
argue that the initiative scapegoats children, lets employers off
the hook, inefficiently enlists public employees to do the work of
the I.N.S. and violates several federal mandates as well as a Supreme Court decision granting all children the right to free education. That several of the state's major newspapers and a cross
section of city governments, school districts, health associations

[2]Article by Elizabeth Kadetsky, a Los Angeles-based free-lance writer, from *The
Nation* 259:416, 418, 420–22 O 17 '94. Copyright © 1994 by The Nation Company,
L.P. Reprinted with permission.

and law-enforcement officials have opposed Save Our State as racist, xenophobic, ineffectual, costly—and just meanspirited— would seem enough to disqualify the avuncular Goodman from its sponsor's ranks.

But Goodman is not alone among Californians, who have responded to the plummeting indicators in almost every measure of quality of life by turning their bitter gaze toward the nation's undocumented immigrants, 43 percent of whom land in California. It's no news that California—strapped by the country's second-weakest economy, four years of budget shortfalls, the most crowded classrooms in the nation and pockets of the worst smog and traffic—is no longer the "golden door" the Grateful Dead still sometimes sing about.

Discontent at the condition of the Golden State has exploded in the faces of immigrants, particularly those from Latin America. The American Friends Service Committee border monitoring project investigates two or three incidents of anti-immigrant violence per month. This atmosphere of panic owes its fire to a network of several dozen mostly new grass-roots organizations whose work, fanned by the goading rhetoric of politicians like incumbent Governor Pete Wilson, has culminated with S.O.S. The authors of S.O.S. have so successfully tapped into a popular sentiment and movement that the group's P.O. box collects as many as 1,000 pieces of mail a day. S.O.S. has had no trouble recruiting volunteers, and those volunteers had an equally easy ride gathering 400,000 of the signatures needed to qualify the initiative for the ballot.

A grass-roots mobilization of this scale stands out sharply against, say, that of Philip Morris, which paid a famously uninformed army of signature-gatherers $1.7 million to qualify its smoking initiative for this year's California ballot. In an election in which gubernatorial candidates are expected to spend $25 million each, S.O.S. had raised only $336,000 by June 30, [1994], less than any other initiative campaign on the ballot. Nearly a quarter of the S.O.S. total was in contributions smaller than $100.

Also unlike the corporate maneuverers behind the bulk of the season's initiatives, S.O.S.'s core supporters are a ragtag movement replete with registered Greens, Democrats, Perotists, distributors of New Age healing products and leaders of the Republican Party. The participants have little in common, but their rhetoric of invasion—a kaffeeklatsch in the Southern California town of Bellflower calls itself We Stand Ready—and the virulence of their wrath. One S.O.S. organizer, Bette Hammond, drove me through her town's immigrant quarter ranting about an imagined "stench of urine" and pointing to clusters of streetside day laborers who, she asserted, surely defecated in the nearby bushes. "Impacted, impacted, impacted," Hammond spit out as she glanced toward apartment complexes in various states of disrepair. "They come here, they have their babies, and after that they become citizens and all those children use those social services." Barbara Kiley, a Prop[osition] 187 backer, who is also mayor of the Orange County town of Yorba Linda, described such children to one reporter as "those little fuckers."

More established right-wing figures have shown up to exploit such sentiments and give mileage to the initiative. In a previously unreported link to the Christian right, Rob Hurtt, a millionaire state senator from Santa Ana, has backed S.O.S. with a $15,000 loan through his business, Container Supply Corporation. Hurtt, who is among S.O.S.'s top six contributors, is also one of four deep pockets behind Allied Business PAC, a funding juggernaut that pumped $3 million into the state's 1992 elections and placed fifteen right-wing Christians in the state legislature.

Richard Mountjoy, a finger-jabbing right-wing Republican state assemblyman from east L.A. County, took up the anti-immigrant torch when, he told me, he foresaw "a heated campaign" for re-election in 1992. He has since become the movement's most tenacious government spokesman, introducing ten mostly unsuccessful bills in the state legislature that foreshadowed Prop[osition] 187 (one would make it a felony to use a false ID). This year Mountjoy one-upped even Prop[osition] 187 with a pending bill that would disqualify native-born children of undocumented mothers from their Fourteenth Amendment right to U.S. citizenship. A self-proclaimed "expert" on immigration, Mountjoy told me he wanted a crackdown on illegal immigration from countries other than Mexico, such as Puerto Rico, where, unbeknownst to the assemblyman, everyone is a U.S. citizen. Mountjoy, who has contributed $43,000 to S.O.S., has cynically blamed immigrants for the state's budget crisis after having built his own career campaigning for Proposition 13, the 1978 antitax initiative that is now acknowledged by experts on all sides as the *actual* cause of that crisis. Other top backers include Don Rogers, a state senator from outside Palm Springs who kicked in $20,000 and is perhaps best known for his association with the white supremacist Christian Identity movement.

Mountjoy and Rogers are not alone in lending the movement for S.O.S. a racist patina. The measure is backed by the Federation for American Immigration Reform (FAIR), an outgrowth of the environmentally leaning Zero Population Growth that has received at least $800,000 from the Pioneer Fund, a notorious right-wing philanthropy that sponsors studies on topics like race and I.Q.

While endorsing the measure, FAIR spokesman Ira Mehlman now distances his group from the S.O.S. organization. Harold Ezell, an S.O.S. co-author, corroborates Mehlman's ambivalence by bitterly noting that FAIR "never gave a dime" to S.O.S. But FAIR's direct link to S.O.S. comes in the person of Alan Nelson, a former I.N.S. director with a WASPishly telegenic presence who wrote Mountjoy's bills along with other anti-immigrant legislation while working for FAIR in the state capital last year. When FAIR chose not to renew Nelson's contract this May, Nelson cannibalized those bills to create S.O.S. "We want to demagnetize the draw for illegal aliens," Nelson told me icily in his office . . . [in 1993].

Nelson and Ezell have since disassociated themselves from S.O.S.'s kooky day-to-day custodians, but they continue to campaign for the measure and have co-founded an organization that plans to export Proposition 187 to other states. For their part, both were key figures in the Reagan Administration I.N.S.—Nelson was its director and Ezell was Western Regional Chief—at the time of two scathing General Accounting Office reports and a Justice Department investigation that criticized the agency for political favoritism in admitting immigrants, overhiring of Border Patrol guards and disorganization.

Ezell now runs a consulting firm that among other things arranges relocations to Southern California for Korean and Taiwanese garment manufacturers—an industry chronically dependent on undocumented labor.

If S.O.S.'s visible advocates personify either fringe populism or cynical manipulation of public sentiment for political gain, their movement has crossed over to the mainstream. Sixty-two percent of Californians supported S.O.S. in a September *Los Angeles Times* poll; however, voters' visceral reaction fades when asked in other polls about the particulars of the proposition, such as yanking children from public schools or denying medical care, which are opposed by 54 percent and 74 percent, respectively. Still, the initiative is expected to pass.

Despite the verbiage about immigrants' economic impact, polls show supporters span the political and economic spectrums and are not more likely to have been adversely affected by the recession. Most of S.O.S.'s support, as well as its most vocal advocates, are actually concentrated in areas least affected by the recession or by the state's shifting multicultural composition.

S.O.S. is most popular in Orange County, the sterile midzone of low-slung shopping malls between border San Diego and multicultural Los Angeles. It's the region that brought us Richard Nixon, Disneyland and S.O.S.'s ten authors. Here, only 7 percent live in poverty, as opposed to 17.5 percent in Los Angeles.

Bette Hammond lives in San Rafael, where she moved from a Boston suburb in 1981, bought a motorcycle and planned "to get the freedom that one hears about from California." For her the dream is this Marin County enclave that is 84 percent white, enjoys the well-above-average median family income of $54,000, the well-below-average unemployment rate of 6 percent—and probably has more hot tubs per capita than any place in the world.

These demographics suggest that Ron Prince, the vampirishly charming chairman of the Save Our State Committee, was disingenuous in recommending as a representative volunteer Parrish Goodman, who is African-American. Goodman likewise planned to illustrate "how the African-American community is organizing around S.O.S."—though he was unable to conjure up one other African-American S.O.S. volunteer besides himself. In fact, anti-immigrant sentiment is concentrated among whites: 59 percent of white people in California believe that children of undocumented immigrants should be turned away from the schools. This contrasts with 41 percent of African-Americans and Asians, and 22 percent of Latinos, according to a Field Institute poll.

A former Black Panther who hails from New York City and is now a union computer technician for the telephone company, Goodman nevertheless exploits black/Latino tensions by harping on a "fight over jobs" in the ethnically volatile African-American and Latino South Central district. Cruising down Venice Boulevard in his white Camaro, Goodman speed-surfed the AM talk-radio channels as his placid surface cracked into little slivers of invective: "These people want you to be like them, poor and mumbling in half-Spanish and half-English." Then Goodman, who came to California in 1980 in search of a "change of attitude," turned calm, almost wistful. "I thought California was supposed to be palm trees and beautiful girls on the beach. Instead we got a gang war. You almost have an enemy presence in your midst."

The backers of S.O.S. believe there is an enemy presence everywhere. Ron Prince speaks of "threats" with the hushed paranoia of a man under siege. He will not divulge the whereabouts of the group's headquarters in Tustin, a sleepy town in Orange County; when asked about the secrecy, Bill Dasher, the one volunteer who works with Prince in their Tustin office, cited "security" problems that had already forced the group to change headquarters.

Prince's mostly bogus claims of harassment include the charge that the Santa Ana Post Office withheld mail for several weeks, accounting for a precipitate decline in the arrival of signed petitions and revealing the hand of an evil "alien" within the Postal Service. The Santa Ana Post Office's Terri Bouffiou responded that an investigation into Prince's charges turned up nothing. The allegation, she added, was "absurd."

Prince is loath to reveal anything about himself other than that he is an accountant and comes from a once-prominent French-American Los Angeles family, but even that admission offers a significant and unreported glimpse into one of the group's many contradictions. Prince, who refers to himself as "about as American as you can get," is in fact the proud descendant of Jean Louis Vignes, who is best remembered in California history for having spurned the Spanish aristocracy by marrying a Mexican-born Indian. This means that Prince's own heritage marks him as an original mestizo harking from the California that was part of Mexico until 1848—the historic link between Mexico and California being one that many see as justification enough for the current movement of Mexicans into the state.

This is an interesting twist because S.O.S. advocates like to interpret the former Mexican ascendance in the Southwest as proof that the Mexican-American War is still going on. Goodman believes all immigrants from Mexico are knowing participants in a "conspiracy" to "take over all this territory that was theirs back in the 1800s." He makes his point by absurdly displaying literature from U.S. (i.e., not Mexican) groups like MEChA, a Chicano student organization, and the newly reborn Chicano nationalist Brown Berets, who do sometimes argue that the real "illegal aliens" invaded Aztlán—the Aztec equivalent of Israel—with Christopher Columbus.

As the rhetoric flies, California does wrestle with the confounding fact that immigrants strain a social and physical infrastructure already burdened by slow economic expansion and a growing population. None of the dozens of wildly contradictory studies circulating among participants in the immigration debate can adequately estimate the real numbers and costs of undocumented immigrants in California, but several concur that while low-wage immigrants contribute to and are even crucial to the state's long-term economic vitality, those immigrants are a short-term burden on state and city governments that cannot, as one study from the RAND Corporation puts it, "borrow against their future." The most resonant of several studies, by Los Angeles County, reported that immigrants (legal and illegal) and their children cost the county $954 million a year in public services but give back far more, $4.3 billion—albeit in taxes paid to the federal government. That discrepancy has led to bipartisan railing against federal mandates—the same mandates that S.O.S. violates—that require states to provide social services without the federal dollars to pay for them. In any case, while S.O.S. ostensibly undoes that burden to the state, the state's legislative analysis has calculated that the measure would actually cost billions in the long run.

Even the cost-benefit equation, however, fails to address the fact that immigration from Mexico is a logical outgrowth of the economic interdependency of Mexico and the United States. State Assembly Speaker Willie Brown did, however, call for seizing the assets of employers such as hoteliers who are found to depend on underpaid and poorly treated undocumented immigrants. This proposal elicited an amusing silence from Republican fist-thumpers like Governor Wilson, who have done everything in their power to see that employer-sanction provisions in the 1986 Immigration Reform and Control Act remain unenforced. After eight years, Los Angeles saw the first major criminal employer sanction doled out this fall.

That a poorly conceived initiative sponsored by fringe activists with a persecution complex will probably win the support of a majority of voters in November points to the willingness of politicians to play the immigration card in a volatile social climate. Viewers watch Pete Wilson television ads that show pandemonium, in wobbly black and white, at the Tijuana/San Diego border checkpoint. It's an image of some fifty people running through the customs gates; it was filmed not during the course of regular affairs but during a one-day border rush that was, for complicated reasons, essentially engineered by the Border Patrol.

Democrats have in general failed at providing leadership to sway the public from its xenophobic frenzy. Senator Barbara Boxer has grandstanded with an illegal proposal to use federal drug interdiction money to dispatch the National Guard to the border—whose militarization has already led to vastly increased human rights violations. Gubernatorial candidate Kathleen Brown and Senator Dianne Feinstein have concurred on calls for a "beefed up" Border Patrol and a $1 border crossing toll—and Feinstein has even indicated she may support S.O.S.

Traditional immigrant advocacy groups have for their part been cowed by the shrillness of the anti-immigrant rhetoric, and groups like the Mexican-American Legal Defense and Education Fund have joined the better-funded of the state's two anti-initiative committees. But Taxpayers Against Proposition 187, an effort of the Republican-leaning P.R. firm Woodward & McDowell, has spent so much energy nodding its head about the presumed "problem" of illegal immigration that individuals like Maria Eraña from the American Friends Service Committee in San Diego have been left with the feeling that "even if Proposition 187 is defeated, the use of these kinds of arguments will be detrimental to all of us afterwards." Eraña and several Latino groups have bristled at Taxpayers' tactics and formed their own Californians Against Proposition 187.

"Everyone is so concerned about keeping the confidence of white people," Eraña added. "They're giving in to all this propaganda. They're concerned that if they take a stand that questions the immigration policies they will be flooded by opposition. If they defend illegal immigrants they will be considered traitors and sellouts."

BEYOND PROPOSITION 187[3]

With the passage of Proposition 187, Californians have put immigration firmly on the national agenda. But today, legal immigration is as much out of control as illegal immigration, with consequences just as troubling. The difference is that it has not

[3]Editorial by Mortimer B. Zuckerman, editor-in-chief of *U.S. News & World Report,* from *U.S. News & World Report* 117:123–4 D 12 '94. Copyright © 1994 by *U.S. News & World Report.* Reprinted with permission.

been politically correct to discuss legal immigration—as if it were somehow reprehensible for Americans to think of controlling the destiny of their country and the integrity of their borders.

The outcry over California's new law shows how hard it is to bring reality to the issue. All illegal immigrants have, by definition, broken the law, and they are guilty of an ethical breach as well: They have jumped the line of people patiently waiting for years for their visas. Liberal opinion believes they should be rewarded for this misconduct—allowed not merely to stay but to freely enjoy the generous education and health care benefits provided by state taxpayers. It is these benefits that 187 denies, except in emergencies. But already the referendum vote is being challenged in the courts. Where is the equity or logic in this? Why should the United States have a duty to house illegal aliens?

But Proposition 187 should be just the starting point. Immigration policy as a whole must be revised, and soon: The temper of the country demands it. Some 65 percent of Americans want fewer immigrants admitted, about double the percentage who felt that way three decades ago, and a stunning 76 percent, anxious about jobs, want immigration reduced until the economy improves. According to one poll, even two thirds of Hispanics believe too many immigrants are entering the country.

The cost of immigration is enormous—$8.4 billion a year, according to a study by the University of Pennsylvania's Wharton School. Earlier eras saw the influx of relatively young, uneducated people willing to take on the farm and factory work in an agricultural nation moving into the industrial age. Like that earlier time, many of today's immigrants are poor and unskilled, especially illegals. What has changed is America: Today, we are a postindustrial state with different needs. In a developing economy, the manual labor immigrants provided was a boon; in modern America, too often, low-skilled newcomers—particularly illegals—are mouths to feed rather than hands to work.

And it's not just a matter of economics. The newer immigrants differ from earlier generations, which were largely from Europe. Latinos, Asians and immigrants from the Caribbean now constitute 80 percent of the yearly influx; many find it hard to leave their own cultures behind and do not easily assimilate. At the same time, American culture has shifted somewhat, from stressing individualism and assimilation to stressing group identity and separatism—a trend that is compounded by affirmative action in education and the workplace. The role of the English language as a unifying force is eroding, too: At vast expense, scores of languages are being used in schools—not so much to enable Americans to converse with foreigners as to preserve the nationalistic ghettos within American society.

Many Americans are rightly concerned that these bilingual, multicultural policies will result in balkanization and the exacerbation of ethnic strife. The situation is worse than the national figures imply because immigrants concentrate near America's gateways. More than 75 percent of all legal immigrants live in six states—California, Florida, Illinois, New York, New Jersey and Texas—and mostly in the centers of cities. Add illegal immigration and that proportion rises to around 90 percent.

How did we get into this mess? It has been thirty years in the making. In 1965, we changed immigration preferences to admit people based on family reunification rather than on their national origin. As a result, immigration shifted from being overwhelmingly European to being overwhelmingly Asian, Latin American and Caribbean; Europeans who had migrated here a long time ago had few additional members coming through family preferences, while Asians and Latin Americans had whole family complexes to import. On top of this, illegal immigration from Latin America shot up to more than 200,000 a year. To address illegal immigration, a new 1986 law offered a deal: Illegals could legalize their status, but further waves of immigration would be stanched by punishing employers if they hired illegals. The primary beneficiaries of this policy have been Latin Americans, especially Mexicans; the 1986 law provided an amnesty for about 2.5 million. And a 1990 law that increased the visas for needed skills maintained the family preference quotas.

The question then remains: Why family preference when it has been even more distorting than national origin as the basis for the bulk of our immigration visas? Now our immigration policy discriminates against Europeans. It should be scrapped and replaced so that we admit more people with high skills and education.

Immigrants today have already contributed to America's tremendous and growing dominance in the industries of the future. One third of the country's engineers and computer chip designers are foreign born; Asians constitute 20 percent or more of America's elite-university student bodies today, and in crucial fields like science and engineering, often half or more are immigrants. A disproportionate number of the student winners of the Westinghouse Science Talent Search come from immigrant families.

This is the kind of immigrant population that should be expanded. Defenders of the present open house argue that the desire to exercise more control over the flow of poor, unskilled immigrants—and to give a preference to those with talents our society wants and needs—is racist or xenophobic. But it is the present patterns that are biased. And none of the people-exporting countries are anywhere nearly as liberal on immigration issues as is the United States. Mexico alone last year deported more than 60,000 undocumented workers.

That is only the beginning of immigration reform. These are some other changes:

• Nonrefugee immigrants who are over 65 should be the responsibility of their sponsors for at least ten years, if not permanently. At present, the sponsors are liable for only three years and then the indigent elderly can file for Supplemental Security Income. Over the last decade, the number of such immigrants receiving SSI has tripled to around 400,000, or 13 percent of all elderly immigrants—about twice the rate at which native-born Americans get SSI. Why should the American taxpayer be providing retirement assistance under these circumstances?

• States should be relieved of the requirement imposed by the Supreme Court to give the same education and nonemergency health care to illegals as they provide to tax-paying citizens. As for legal immigrants, some 60 percent of taxes they pay end up in the hands of the federal government, with 29 percent to the state and only 11 percent to the local community. There should be a redistribution of revenues received or benefits allocated by the federal government so that the states and communities where immigrants concentrate—and that supply most of the public services they use—are not adversely affected.

• Congress should review the eligibility rules for publicly funded programs available to legal resident aliens. The period before these aliens qualify for welfare benefits should be adjusted.

• Our borders must be secured against illegals through increased manpower and resources.

• We should review the number of refugees we allow to enter and our standards for political asylum. The cold war is over.

This review of immigration policy is overdue. The Ellis Island tradition served us well in the past and can again: It allowed through the Golden Door those with willing and able hands and excluded those with illnesses or who were otherwise likely to become a burden on society. Instead of taking a hard look at our policies, however, we temporize. The flood tides keep rolling in, and they will continue to do so as the gap between our standard of living and that of economically marginalized countries continues to grow. If you measure the standard of living in terms of living space per person, food and access to television, the standard of living in a California jail is higher than that in many Latin American villages. The pressures will intensify, and our defenses are down.

Immigration made America what it is. I write as an immigrant myself. I can testify to the generosity of the people and the spirit of the country. America offers great opportunities to everyone who is willing to take advantage of the ethic of individualism, opportunity and hard work and to identify with America's hopes and purposes. When immigration has got out of hand in the past, we have never hesitated to control it. Now it is more than a matter of numbers. The very identity of America is at stake.

WHAT TO DO ABOUT IMMIGRATION[4]

Despite overwhelming opposition from the media, from leaders of the religious and civil-rights communities, from the education establishment, and even from prominent conservatives like Jack Kemp and William J. Bennett, California voters last fall enthusiastically adopted Proposition 187, which bars illegal aliens from receiving welfare, education, or health benefits except for emergency medical treatment.

The anger toward illegal immigrants had grown steadily among Californians in recent years, fueled both by the huge number of illegal aliens living in the state—nearly two million, or about half of the country's entire illegal population—and by the state's lingering economic recession. And the resentment had deepened as the apparent costs of providing benefits to illegal aliens rose; for the fiscal year 1994–95, that figure is estimated to

[4]Article by Linda Chavez, author and president of the Center for Equal Opportunity in Washington, D.C., from *Commentary* 99:29–35 N '95. Copyright © 1995 by *Commentary*. All rights reserved. Reprinted with permission.

stand at $2.35 billion. California, moreover, had gone far beyond what was required by federal law in granting benefits to illegal aliens, including in-state tuition in the Cal-State University system and free prenatal care.

As if all this were not tinder enough, in mid-October 70,000 mostly Latin demonstrators marched through downtown Los Angeles waving Mexican and Guatemalan flags and shouting *Viva la Raza*. Tracking polls, which had shown Proposition 187 ahead by only five points just prior to the demonstration, registered a fourfold jump in the three days immediately following.

Proposition 187's success has inspired activists in several other states to consider similar measures, but their plans may be derailed if the law is declared unconstitutional. (A federal court has enjoined California from enforcing Proposition 187, pending the outcome of a suit.) Nonetheless, the proposal's popularity has launched a long-overdue national debate on immigration—legal as well as illegal.

Like so much American social policy, immigration policy is a monument to the law of unintended consequences. Although assurances to the contrary were offered by the legislators responsible for the last major overhaul of the nation's immigration law, the 1965 Immigration and Nationality Act, that law profoundly altered both the makeup and the size of the immigrant flow. Until 1965, most immigrants came from Europe; today, some 80 percent of those legally admitted are from Asia or Latin America. The new law also significantly increased the pool of eligible applicants by giving preference to family members of immigrants already here.

But these changes might not have had such striking effects had they not coincided with dramatic developments in civil-rights law and with the expansion of the welfare state. As it is, immigration now intersects with two of the most troubling issues of our time: race and entitlements.

In 1993 (the last year for which figures are available), over 800,000 legal immigrants were admitted to the United States and an estimated 300,000 illegal aliens settled here, more or less permanently. Over the last decade, as many as ten million legal and illegal immigrants established permanent residence—a number higher than at any period in our history, including the peak immigration decade of 1900–10.

To be sure, these numbers are somewhat misleading: because our population is so much larger now than it was at the beginning of the century, the rate of immigration is much lower, barely one-third of what it was then. And while the proportion of persons living in the U.S. who are foreign-born is high by recent standards—about 8 percent in the last census—it is still lower than it was for every decade between 1850 and 1950.

The numbers alone, however, do not fully describe the dimensions of the immigration issue. Americans are not just concerned about the size of the immigrant population; they are worried about the kind of people who are coming, how they got here, and whether they are likely to become a benefit or a burden to our society. There is deep suspicion that today's immigrants are fundamentally different from earlier waves. In recent polls, 59 percent of Americans say that immigration was good for the country in the past, but only 29 percent think it is a good thing now. Former Colorado Governor Richard Lamm, who favors restricting immigration, summed up this national ambivalence: "I know that earlier large waves of immigrants didn't 'overturn' America, but there are . . . reasons to believe that today's migration is different from earlier flows."

Immigration enthusiasts (among whom I count myself, albeit with some important reservations) like to point out that Americans have never been eager to accept new arrivals, for all our rhetoric about being an "immigrant nation." As Rita Simon of the American University law school noted recently, "We view immigrants with rose-colored glasses, turned backward." Perhaps, then, there is nothing much new in the worries so many people express about whether this generation of immigrants will indeed assimilate to American norms. But comforting as the thought may be that today's Mexicans, Vietnamese, Pakistanis, and Filipinos are the equivalent of yesterday's Italians, Jews, Poles, and Irish, it fails to take into account the tremendous transformation America itself has undergone in the last half-century.

The America to which Europeans immigrated—first northern Europeans in the 19th century and then southern and eastern Europeans in the first quarter of the 20th—was a self-confident, culturally homogeneous nation. There was never any question that immigrants would be expected to learn English and to conform to the laws, customs, and traditions of their new country (although even then, some immigration restrictionists questioned whether certain groups were capable of such conformity). And immigrants themselves—especially their children—eagerly wanted to adapt. Public schools taught newcomers not only a new language, but new dress, manners, history, myths, and even hygiene to transform them into Americans who sounded, looked, acted, thought, and smelled the part.

In those days there were no advocates insisting that America must accommodate itself to the immigrants; the burden of change rested solely with the new arrivals. To be sure, by their sheer numbers they managed subtly to alter certain features of their new country. Because of them, the U.S. is less Protestant than it would otherwise have been; no doubt American cuisine and art are richer; and the pantheon of American heroes from Christopher Columbus to Joe DiMaggio to Albert Einstein is more diverse. Still, until fairly recently, Americans—native-stock or of later lineage—understood what it meant to be American, and it meant roughly the same thing regardless of where one's ancestors came from.

We are far less sure what it means to be American today. Thus the question, "What to do about immigration?" is inextricably wound up with how we define our national identity.

Some critics of immigration—most notably John O'Sullivan, the editor of *National Review,* and Peter Brimelow, author of the forthcoming *Alien Nation*—believe that national identity must be defined in explicitly racial and ethnic terms and that the current high levels of nonwhite immigration will drastically alter that identity. O'Sullivan argues:

A nation is an ethno-cultural unit—a body that begins its life as a cultural in-gathering but, by dint of common history, habits, tastes, shared experiences, tales, songs, memories, and, above all, intermarriage, becomes progressively more like an extended family—that is, more ethnic—over time.

As long as America's core remained overwhelmingly Wasp, so this argument goes, it was possible for Italian Catholics or Russian Jews or Japanese Buddhists to become American. Both O'Sullivan and Brimelow fear, however, that the large numbers of nonwhites who are now coming in will undermine the assimilative capacity of the nation; they both cite Census Bureau projections that the majority of the U.S. population will become nonwhite (or more accurately, non-Hispanic white) by the year 2050; and they both blame current immigration policy for this portentous outcome.

But is race or ethnicity really the issue? If so, O'Sullivan and Brimelow can relax. Yes, the majority of immigrants admitted to the U.S. in the last twenty years have been relatively dark-skinned Mexicans, Filipinos, Vietnamese, Chinese, Koreans, etc. Yet by the year 2050, their great grandchildren are unlikely to look like them. Intermarriage rates in the U.S. have never been higher; nor have mixed-race births. The Population Reference Bureau (PRB) recently touted this development in its monthly newsletter in a front-page article, "Interracial Baby Boomlet in Progress?" Births to mixed Japanese/white couples now exceed those to all-Japanese couples. There are now so many ethnically-mixed persons in the U.S. that the Census Bureau is debating whether to create a special classification for them. (Perhaps it should consider calling the category "American.") Not even groups with strong traditions or religious prohibitions against intermarriage seem exempt from the trend. About half of all American Jews, for example, marry non-Jews.

Nor is the inclination to intermarry diminishing among more recent immigrant groups. One-third of young, U.S.-born Hispanics marry non-Hispanics; and perhaps more significantly, nearly half of all Hispanics consider themselves white. Peter Brimelow dismisses this phenomenon, noting that those of Mexican origin, who make up nearly two-thirds of the entire group, are predominantly Indian. But he misses the point. By defining themselves as white, Hispanics are identifying with the majority. In a recent survey, a majority of Hispanics said the group with which they felt they had most in common was whites, and so did Asians.

In short, the problem of national identity is not primarily connected with heredity or ethnicity. It is, rather, a function of culture. But on this score, the evidence is decidedly less re-assuring.

From the White House to Madison Avenue to Main Street, the idea has taken hold that the United States is a multicultural society. Many doubt that such a thing as American culture even exists. When I recently told a university audience that American blacks, Hispanics, Asians, and whites have more in common with one another than they do with their contemporaries in any of their ancestral homelands, the students literally gasped in disbelief. "I don't know what you mean by 'American culture,'" one young Puerto Rican woman told me. "I have a right to my own culture and language." She said this, however, in perfect English, leaving me wondering just what culture and language she might be referring to.

But if the irony of her situation escaped this particular student—whose coloring and features suggested predominantly Spanish ancestry—her political statement was clear. A European-looking, English-speaking Hispanic who chooses to reject American culture, she represents the flip side of the large number of brown-skinned Hispanics who see themselves as white. It is hard to know how many such persons there are, but their numbers are surely growing as ethnicity becomes increasingly politicized.

Into this confusing mix come immigrants who, unlike these *ersatz* ethnics, truly are culturally different from those around them. And such are the misgivings of the rest of us that we no longer seem able or willing to help these newcomers become Americans. Public schools, which worked to acculturate previous immigrant groups, now see it as their mission to preserve immigrant languages and culture. The Los Angeles school system, which educates more Latino immigrant children than any in the nation, prides itself on teaching these youngsters primarily in Spanish for three years or more. Denver public-school officials recently ordered one local high school to stop teaching 450 Hispanic youngsters in English, and transferred out fifty-one Asian students so that the school could concentrate on its Spanish bilingual program. The demand for Spanish-speaking teachers is so great that districts from Los Angeles to Chicago have begun importing instructors from Mexico, Spain, and Puerto Rico; in 1993, Mexico signed an agreement with California to provide both teachers and 40,000 textbooks for the state's Spanish-language classrooms.

Yet bilingual education did not originally grow out of the pressures of immigration. It started as a small, federally funded program to help Mexican-American children (largely native-born) in the Southwest, and it was already in place years before the large influx of Spanish-speaking immigrants in the 1970's and 80's. Its chief sponsor, former Senator Ralph Yarborough (D-Tex), declared that the purpose of his bilingual-education bill was not "to create pockets of different languages throughout the country . . . but just to try to make [Mexican-American] children fully literate in English." By 1975, however, civil-rights enforcement agencies in Washington were insisting (on the basis of a Supreme Court ruling involving the Civil Rights Act of 1964) that school districts teach "language-minority" youngsters, mostly Mexican-Americans and Puerto Ricans, in Spanish or face a cut-off of all federal funds.

In the early stages of the program, the overwhelming majority of students in bilingual classes were U.S.-born; today, nearly 60 percent still are. What is more, many of these children are more fluent in English than Spanish—no one knows exactly how many, because most states use an arbitrary cut-off score (usually the 30th or 40th percentile) on a standardized English test to place Hispanic youngsters in Spanish-language programs, rather than testing to see whether they are more fluent in English or in Spanish.

Bilingual voting ballots, which are now mandated by the federal government, were also an outgrowth not of immigration but of civil-rights legislation—in this case, the 1975 Amendments to the Voting Rights Act of 1965—and they too were aimed at a U.S.-born population: namely, Mexican-Americans living in the Southwest. The main impetus behind the amendments was to give Washington the same power to oversee federal elections in areas where Hispanics lived as the original Act gave it over the Deep South, where egregious efforts were being made to prevent blacks from voting.

Since few Spanish-speaking immigrants naturalize and since few can therefore vote, the 1975 amendments have had little effect on them. But thanks to additional amendments adopted in 1982, and a series of court decisions, the Voting Rights Act is now used mainly to create districts which pack in as many Hispanics (or blacks) as feasible in order to assure the election of minority candidates. This practice has received widespread publicity because of the often bizarrely gerrymandered districts that result, but what is less well-known is that immigrants—including illegal aliens—often make up the majority of persons entitled to representation in these new Hispanic districts.

So far, at least, the Act has not been invoked to create safe districts for Asians, although in principle they qualify under the same "language-minority" designation as Hispanics. The law already requires federal ballots to be printed in Chinese, Vietnamese, and Korean, among other languages; and the huge increase in the Asian immigrant population in California probably means that the courts will before long use their presence to justify the need for safe seats for Asians. Since Asians are too widely dispersed for simple ethnic gerrymandering to suffice, we may expect the courts to order new remedies such as cumulative voting. This technique, which allows voters to cast multiple ballots for a single candidate in a multimember, at-large race, would, for example, enable Asians comprising only 14 percent of the electorate in a given city to elect one representative on a six-member city council even if no whites voted for the Asian candidate.

The manipulation of both the Bilingual Education Act and

the Voting Rights Act points to a central problem of our present immigration policy: the current confluence of ethnic-based entitlements and the large influx of newcomers eligible to receive them creates an ever-growing demand for such programs.

One solution, favored by those who want to restrict immigration for other reasons, is to cut off the flow of immigrants. Yet while this might diminish the clientele for ethnic entitlements, the programs would continue to serve the native-born populations for whom they were originally created. For it is not immigrants who clamor for these programs. Asian immigrants, for one, have largely eschewed bilingual education in favor of English-immersion programs. Even some Latino immigrant parents have staged protests in California, New York, and New Jersey upon discovering that their children were being taught in Spanish; others simply withdraw their children, sending them to parochial schools that teach all students in English.

The other solution to the problem of ethnic entitlements, of course, would be simply to end them for everyone. There are many good reasons for doing this, even if immigration were to cease altogether. Race- and ethnic-based entitlements have been a bane of American social policy for the last quarter-century. They have divided Americans, increased group hostility, and perverted the whole notion of color-blind justice. Furthermore, they are the foundation on which the entire edifice of multiculturalism is built. Without the enticement of racial and ethnic preferences in education, employment, voting, and elsewhere, group identity, instead of intensifying in recent years, might have diminished.

Multicultural education has become the main instrument to help preserve group identity. But multicultural education is no more a byproduct of increased Latin and Asian immigration than are bilingual education and ballots, ethnic voting districts, and affirmative action. In fact, multicultural education first came into being largely to address the demands of blacks for proportional representation in the curriculum—though by now it has spread (some would say, metastasized) to the point where all students are encouraged to think of themselves primarily as members of groups rather than as Americans.

Thus, when California recently adopted a new textbook series for kindergarten through eighth grade, ethnic protestors turned out at schoolboard hearings in San Francisco, Los Angeles, San Diego, Oakland, and other cities, insisting upon changes not only in the treatment of blacks but also in the way the series dealt with

Indians, Hispanics, Jews, Muslims, and even conservative Christians.

Critics of immigration like O'Sullivan and Brimelow believe that multiculturalism would, in O'Sullivan's words, "be easier to dismantle if immigration were reduced." But the California story suggests that, if anything, it is ethnic diversity itself that might actually hasten the demise of multiculturalism. Like a house of cards that has grown too unwieldy, multicultural education may collapse of its own weight if it is required to include the distinct stories of each of the hundreds of different groups now in the schools.

But the unraveling of multicultural education, salutary a prospect as it may be, is hardly a good reason for maintaining our current immigration policy. Clearly, that policy needs changing in ways that are consistent with our national interests and values. I would argue, indeed, that our immigration policy should *reinforce* our national identity—which is not necessarily the same thing as our racial or ethnic composition. What, then, should we do? Let me deal with legal immigration first.

Change the System to One that Favors Skills

The basis of the current system is the principle of family reunification, adopted in 1965 with the expectation that this would maintain the ethnic balance of the U.S. population as it existed at the time. Of course things have not worked out that way. But questions of ethnic balance aside, there is nothing sacrosanct about family reunification as a guiding principle of immigration policy, and we should not be deterred from changing it out of fear that such a move might be interpreted as racist.

In any case, the problem with the current immigrant pool is not that there are too many Latinos and Asians *per se,* but that too many of the people we now admit are low-skilled. Mexicans come with only about seven years of schooling on average, and less than a quarter have obtained high-school diplomas. Such newcomers face a much more difficult period of adjustment and bring fewer benefits to the U.S. economy than would more highly skilled immigrants.

It is true that under current criteria, which include only 140,000 slots for skills-based admissions, immigrants are twice as likely to hold Ph.D.'s as are U.S.-born persons. But they are also more likely to be high-school drop-outs. We ought to admit more of the former and fewer of the latter, and regardless of their country of origin. As it turns out, immigrants from Africa and Asia have among the highest average levels of education. Nearly 90 percent of all African immigrants are high-school graduates—a figure 15-percent higher than that for Canadian immigrants. And Indians, Taiwanese, and Iranians have among the highest proportions of college or graduate degrees.

Encourage Immigrants to Assimilate

Immigration policy entails more than laws regulating who gets admitted and under what criteria. It also involves—or at least should involve—how we incorporate immigrants into our society. On that score, we are doing much more poorly now than we did in the past, in part because we have given up on the notion that we have an obligation to assimilate immigrants. Regardless of what other changes we make in immigration policy, we must reverse course on this issue. If immigration to the U.S. ceased tomorrow, we would still have twenty million foreign-born persons living here, plus their children. Assimilation is essential for them, as well as for the rest for us, if we are to stop the further fragmenting of our society.

First and foremost, this means encouraging immigrants and their children to learn English, which in practical terms means abolishing bilingual education in favor of English-immersion programs in the public schools. By now we have nearly thirty years of experience demonstrating that bilingual education helps children neither to learn English nor to do better in school. Latino immigrants in particular have been badly served by bilingual education—and by their putative leaders, usually U.S.-born, who are the main lobby behind this expensive, ineffective, and wasteful program.

But bilingual education is not the only culprit. With so many services available in their native language, immigrants have fewer incentives today to learn English than they did in the past. Private services—native-language newspapers, advertising, etc.—fall outside the scope of public policy. But *government* services ought to be provided only in English. A common language has been critical to our success in forging a sense of national identity. Our public policies should preserve and protect that heritage. If the courts continue to obstruct local and state efforts to make English the official language of government, we should pass a federal constitutional amendment to ensure it.

Limit Welfare Benefits

Although immigrants as a whole are somewhat more likely than natives to receive welfare, the opposite is true of those of working age (15–64). In addition, immigrants have higher labor-force-participation rates than natives, with Hispanic men having among the highest—83.4 percent compared with 75 percent for non-Hispanic whites. If we modify our admission criteria to favor more highly skilled immigrants, welfare among working-age immigrants should drop below even the current rate of about 3 percent, alleviating much of the concern about immigrants and welfare.

The problem is high dependency rates among refugees and elderly immigrants. Among the former, this is a direct result of U.S. policy, which guarantees cash and medical assistance to all persons admitted under the refugee-resettlement program. Having been admitted, they are then attracted to states with relatively high benefits, and this tends to encourage long-term dependency. Thus, in California, some two-thirds of Laotian and Cambodian refugees and more than one-third of Vietnamese refugees remain on welfare after more than five years in the U.S.

While dealing comprehensively with this situation entails the much larger issue of welfare reform, it is possible to make a dent in it by redesigning programs to limit the number of months refugees can receive assistance. One of the most promising possibilities would be to turn over responsibility for such assistance to private agencies, such as Catholic Charities, Lutheran Immigration and Refugee Service, and the Council of Jewish Federations, which have proved more successful at moving refugees off welfare. In Chicago, 74 percent of refugees in an experimental private resettlement project found work within six months of arrival, and only 2 percent remained on welfare after thirteen months, compared with more than 40 percent in the state-administered program.

The problem of elderly immigrants is more complicated. In 1990, 55 percent of elderly Chinese immigrants in California who had arrived between 1980 and 1987 were on welfare, as were 21 percent of elderly Mexican immigrants. Because they have worked too few years or at insufficient wages to qualify for adequate Social Security benefits, most such recipients obtain Supplemental Security Income (SSI).

But many of these immigrants are the parents of resident

aliens who brought them here under family-reunification provisions. Anyone who sponsors an immigrant must guarantee that he will not become a public burden, and is required to accept full financial responsibility for up to five years. Simply enforcing these provisions would greatly alleviate the problem of welfare dependency among elderly immigrants. (Among recipients in California that should not pose a problem, since 50 percent of their children's households in 1990 had incomes over $50,000, and 11 percent over $100,000.) We might also consider lengthening the number of years sponsors are required to provide support to family members; Canada currently requires a ten-year commitment.

All these reforms are addressed to the policies governing legal immigration. What about illegal immigration?

Like welfare dependency among immigrants, illegal immigration is not so big a problem as many people imagine (in one recent poll, two-thirds said they thought most immigrants are illegal aliens). Estimates of overall numbers vary widely, with some commentators hysterically claiming more than ten million illegal aliens. But the more reliable Census Bureau estimates about four million, with (as noted earlier) another 300,000 or so added each year.

In theory, no amount of illegal immigration is acceptable, since the phenomenon represents our failure to maintain secure borders, a prerequisite of national sovereignty. In practice, however, it is unlikely that we will ever completely eradicate illegal immigration: our borders are too long and porous and our society too free and prosperous. But there are steps we can take that would significantly reduce the current flow.

• **Stop illegal aliens at the border.** There is no mainstream support for mass round-ups and deportations of the type used in the 1930's and 50's to roust illegal aliens; nor could such a program withstand legal challenge. Therefore, the only way to reduce the flow is to contain it at the border. The frontier between Mexico and the U.S. is 2,000 miles long, but only about 250 miles of it are traversable. Most illegal aliens enter in a handful of places near metropolitan areas—about 65 percent around San Diego and El Paso.

We know that it is possible to reduce the flow significantly with more Immigration and Naturalization Service (INS) personnel and better equipment and technology. A recent two-month, $25-million experiment in beefed-up border control near San Diego halved the number of illegal crossings; similar experiments in El

Paso produced comparable results. While the most determined may seek alternative routes of entry, for the large majority rough terrain will limit the opportunity.

• **Deport alien criminals.** Apprehending and deporting illegal aliens who have successfully gotten past the border requires more resources and more draconian enforcement measures than most Americans would be willing to endorse; but there is overwhelming support for deporting those arrested for criminal acts in the U.S. In order to do this, however, local law-enforcement officials must be able to ascertain the status of persons in their custody, which they cannot now do easily. A pilot program in Phoenix, which allows police officers 24-hour access to INS records, might prove an effective model for enhancing local police efforts and making more deportations feasible.

• **Outlaw sanctuaries.** Several cities, including San Francisco, Sacramento, and Chicago, have enacted ordinances banning city employees from contacting the INS if they know someone is in the country illegally. These ordinances are an outrage and show utter disregard for the rule of law. Any city that chooses to obstruct immigration enforcement should lose all federal funds.

• **Deny welfare benefits to illegal aliens.** This is what California voters thought they were enacting with Proposition 187. In fact, in most states illegal aliens are already prohibited from receiving welfare and any but emergency medical treatment, but the authorities lack adequate means to verify the legal status of recipients. Consequently, a pilot program instituted in the early 1980's, the Alien Status Verification Index, should be expanded and upgraded with access to on-line INS data bases so that the status of welfare recipients can be checked.

A potentially more intractable problem is that U.S.-born children of illegal aliens are eligible, as citizens, for AFDC and other welfare benefits. Indeed, one out of four new AFDC recipients in California is a child of illegal-alien parents. The only way to prevent them from receiving benefits is to deny them citizenship in the first place, which would probably require a constitutional amendment. I would not suggest that we travel this route, at least not until we have exhausted all other means of keeping illegal aliens out. But neither should we consider the mere discussion of the issue taboo, as it is in most public-policy circles today. Especially now, when U.S. citizenship entails many more rights and benefits than responsibilities, it should not be beyond the pale to reconsider what entitles a person to obtain it.

• **Repeal employer sanctions.** While we are looking at ways to prevent illegal immigration, we ought to acknowledge that the linchpin of our current policy—punishing the employers of illegal aliens—has been a miserable failure. The Immigration Reform and Control Act of 1986, which established such sanctions, did virtually nothing to reduce the flow into the country. If anything, it probably contributed to the problem of welfare dependency among the four million illegal aliens already here, by making it more difficult for them to support themselves.

In typical fashion, those who falsely promised that employer sanctions would fix the illegal-alien problem now think they can tinker with the existing provisions to make it work. Senator Alan Simpson proposes a national identity card; the U.S. Commission on Immigration Reform thinks a national computerized work registry will do the trick.

But the purpose of both would be to enable employers to become better policemen for the immigration system, when they should never have been put in that position in the first place. Nor should the rest of us have to put up with more regulations and infringements on our privacy. It is simply wrong to burden the 98.5 percent of persons who are legally in the country with cumbersome and probably ineffective new requirements in order to try to punish the 1.5 percent of persons who have no right to be here.

These recommendations probably will not satisfy the most ardent foes of immigration, like the Federation for American Immigration Reform (FAIR), the most influential restrictionist organization now operating. But many restrictionists are confused or just plain wrong about the nature of the immigration problem.

FAIR, for example, focuses almost exclusively on two issues: the size of current immigration, and its economic consequences. But neither of these is the heart of the matter.

FAIR's roots are in the population-control and environmentalist movements: this explains its preoccupation with numbers. Its founder, John Tanton, is a past president of Zero Population Growth and chairman of the National Sierra Club Population Committee. FAIR's two most prominent demographer-gurus are Garrett Hardin and Leon Bouvier, both of whom have been actively involved with population-control groups. Their primary concern is that immigrants—no matter where they are from or what their social and economic characteristics—add to the size of the population. (Bouvier has actually said that he believes the ideal U.S. population would be 150 million persons, though he has not clearly spelled out what he would do with the other 100 million of us who are already here.)

It is true that immigrants account for about half of current population growth in the U.S. Nonetheless, U.S. population growth as a whole is relatively modest, at 1 percent per year. Even with immigrants, including the more fecund Latins, we are in no danger of a Malthusian population explosion.

FAIR's other chief concern, the economic impact of immigration, probably has more resonance in the general debate; but here, too, confusion reigns. For years economists have discussed the consequences of immigration—legal and illegal—without coming to a definitive consensus. On one side are those like Julian Simon of the University of Maryland, who argue that immigration is a big plus for the economy, actually improving the standard of living of the native-born. At the other end of the spectrum are those like Donald Huddle of Rice University, the author of an influential 1993 study for the Carrying Capacity Network, a population-control group in Washington. Huddle estimates that immigrants (legal and illegal) cost more than $42.5 billion a year in net public assistance and displace more than two million American workers, incurring $12 billion a year in additional public-assistance costs for those displaced.

Huddle's figures have been widely disputed, including most recently in a General Accounting Office study. Even George Borjas of the University of California, San Diego, easily the most influential academic critic of current policy, estimates that immigration brings economic benefits to the U.S. in the range of $6 to $20 billion annually—small, but still a net positive gain. More importantly, Borjas acknowledges that these benefits could be increased significantly if we changed our policy to attract more skilled immigrants.

No economic model, however, can adequately capture the more subtle benefits that Americans have clearly derived from immigration, and not just from the flows that brought many of our grandparents and great-grandparents here. As Francis Fukuyama and others have argued, most immigrants still seem to personify the very traits we think of as typically American: optimism, ambition, perseverance—the qualities that have made this country great. The ranks of successful immigrant entrepreneurs are legion; in Silicon Valley alone, recent immigrants have built many of the major technology companies, including Sun Microsystems, AST, and Borland International.

Immigrants have also transformed urban America over the

last decade, from Korean grocers in New York to Salvadoran busboys and janitors in Washington, Mexican babysitters and construction workers in Los Angeles, Cambodian doughnut-shop owners in Long Beach, Haitian cooks in Miami, Russian taxi drivers in Philadelphia, and Filipino nurses and Indian doctors in public hospitals practically everywhere. As they always have done, immigrants still take the difficult, often dirty, low-paying, thankless jobs that other Americans shun. When they open their own businesses, these are frequently located in blighted, crime-ridden neighborhoods long since abandoned by American enterprise. And their children often outperform those who have been here for generations. This year, as in the last several, more than one-third of the finalists in the Westinghouse high-school science competition bore names like Chen, Yu, Dasgupta, Khazanov, Bunyavanich, and Hattangadi.

The contrast between the immigrant poor and the American underclass is especially striking. As the sociologist William Julius Wilson and others have observed, Mexican immigrants in Chicago, despite their relative poverty and much lower levels of education, show few of the dysfunctional characteristics of unemployment, crime, welfare dependency, and drug use common among the city's black and Puerto Rican underclass. In cities like Los Angeles and Washington, where American blacks and Latino immigrants inhabit the same poor neighborhoods, the despair of the former seems all the more intense by contrast to the striving of the latter—as if one group had given up on America even as the other was proving the continued existence of opportunity.

For all our anxiety about immigrants, then, in the end it is Americans of all classes who are caught in the middle of a national identity crisis. It is still possible to turn immigrants into what St. John de Crèvecoeur called "a new race of men," provided the rest of us still want to do this. But if we, the affluent no less than the poor among us, cease to believe that being an American has any worth or meaning, we should not blame immigrants, most of whom entertain no such doubts.

GIULIANI CRITICIZES A U.S. CRACKDOWN ON ILLEGAL ALIENS[5]

Immigration restrictions gathering steam in the Republican-led Congress would have "catastrophic social effects" in New York City and other large cities, Mayor Rudolph W. Giuliani said yesterday. He charged that the proposals violated basic decency and could throw as many as 60,000 immigrant children out of the city's schools and onto the streets.

Once again taking sharp exception with the dominant conservative wing of his own party, Mr. Giuliani said in an interview that the proposed crackdown on illegal immigrants was deliberately intended to play to the public's worst fears of foreigners, and did not take into consideration the positive effects of immigrants on cities like New York.

"It's based on an irrational fear of something different, something strange, that somehow they're going to take something away from us," he said. "A lot of it is just undifferentiated fear of foreigners, of people who appear to have different values or different ways of doing things."

In June, the Congressional Task Force on Immigration Reform, a Republican-dominated panel appointed by Speaker Newt Gingrich, issued a report containing dozens of recommendations on restricting illegal immigration.

The proposals, now being written into bills that are at various stages of consideration in House committees, would require public hospitals to report illegal aliens who seek medical treatment and would require public schools to turn away students who are in this country illegally. The report, which Mr. Gingrich endorsed, is similar to Proposition 187, a measure approved by California voters last November that would cut off most public benefits to illegal aliens.

Mr. Giuliani, a grandson of Italian immigrants, said the proposals would be both morally and fiscally devastating to cities, which would suddenly be put in the position of enforcing national immigration laws that the Federal Government has failed to implement.

[5]Article by David Firestone, *New York Times* staff writer, from *New York Times* Al + Ag 23 '95. Copyright © 1995 by New York Times Company. Reprinted with permission.

The city's public schools, for example, have between 40,000 and 60,000 students whose parents are undocumented aliens, he said. If the Board of Education were forced to search for and report those families, he said, many of the parents would simply not send their children to school, resulting in tens of thousands of children on the street, driving up crime and putting both the children and other residents in danger.

Illegal aliens might also be scared away from public hospitals if a similar reporting requirement were used there, he said, even if the hospitals would be allowed to provide emergency care. That could result in an increase of communicable diseases, he said, and would be morally wrong.

"It's just out of a sense of decency," he said. "I can't imagine, even in parts of the country where the views are harsher than they might be in New York, that they're basically going to say, let people die."

One of the architects of Mr. Gingrich's immigration policy accused the Mayor of pandering.

"It's a sad day when you have a person with Rudy Giuliani's credentials, someone who has dedicated his life to the criminal justice system, openly advocating protecting those who are violating the law," said Representative Elton Gallegly, a California Republican who is chairman of the immigration task force. "Unlike Mayor Giuliani, I make no apologies for putting Americans first."

Under an executive order signed by Mayor Edward I. Koch in 1985 and still in effect, city agencies are required to provide services to illegal immigrants and are prohibited from turning over information or any immigrant to the Federal Immigration and Naturalization Service unless the immigrant has been charged with a crime.

The House task force, comprising forty-six Republicans and eight Democrats, includes only one member from New York State, Representative Susan Molinari, a Republican from Staten Island. She was out of the country yesterday and unavailable for comment.

Mr. Gallegly said the school requirement was no more burdensome than verification of residency to attend a neighborhood school. He said that if taxpayers were going to continue paying for the medical care of illegal aliens in emergency rooms, then the Government has the right to know who those patients are so they can be deported.

Mr. Gallegly, who represents Ventura County, near Los Angeles, stressed that the measures would only apply to illegal aliens, not other immigrants who have entered the country legally. But other legislation in the House would take benefits away even from legal immigrants.

*Giuliani Sees an Increase in Truancy and Crime Resulting
from a Federal Bill*

In March, the House passed a welfare bill that would deny food stamps, Medicaid and welfare payments to legal residents of the country who are not citizens.

A comparable welfare bill introduced in the Senate by the majority leader, Bob Dole, would allow states to cut off benefits to legal aliens, but would not require them to do so.

Mr. Giuliani said that the welfare proposal, if enacted into law, would cost the city millions of dollars. Though his administration has been removing thousands of people from the local welfare rolls through heightened scrutiny of their applications, he said the city was not prepared to take care of thousands of aliens who would lose Federal benefits and become destitute.

"This is an absolute shifting of responsibility to city and state governments that can do nothing about the immigration problem," he said. "And I think it's the worst kind of Federal scapegoating."

The Mayor said he plans to work quietly with other mayors, and allies in Congress, to prevent the provisions from becoming law. Last year, he said, he joined successful lobbying to remove two provisions that would have had a similarly negative effect on New York City: the crime bill would have required cities to turn in the names of all illegal aliens discovered from all sources, including people who report crimes, and the education bill would have required schools to determine if all parents were legal residents.

Noting that the immigration issue has divided the leadership of the Republican Party, Mr. Giuliani said the restrictive proposals violate one of the party's most basic principles, which he described as "government acts best when it acts least." He said the proposals also fail to take note of the important economic effects of immigration on such New York neighborhoods as Flushing, Queens, which during the last few decades has been transformed by waves of Chinese and Korean immigrants.

"From the point of view of pure dollars and cents, the notion that immigrants are taking away opportunities and taking away jobs from other people largely isn't the case," he said. "They're creating opportunities, and creating an area of commerce that otherwise just wouldn't happen."

IV. THE IMMIGRATION POLICY DEBATE

EDITOR'S INTRODUCTION

Section Four presents the conflicting views of various spokesmen in the immigration policy debate. In a book review reprinted from the *Atlantic,* Jack Miles notes that the Immigration and Nationality Act Amendments of 1965, which ended national quotas and introduced the family-reunification principle, assumed that there would be no dramatic increase in immigration or in the ethnic make up of the U. S. population—assumptions that proved to be seriously in error. Miles's discussion, centers around Peter Brimelow's recent, much talked about book, *Alien Nation,* which lays out the conservative position on immigration. Miles has reservations, but agrees with Brimelow that American immigration law needs to be reformed "severely and quickly."

Peter Skerry's article in *Commentary* is also a book review on Brimelow's book, which favors doubling the size of the Border Patrol; reviving Operation Wetback, the 1954 effort that rounded up and deported thousands of illegal Mexican nationals; terminating all public benefits to all illegals; and canceling affirmative action benefits to immigrants whatever their status. The next article, by Jacob Weisberg in *New York,* attacks Brimelow's views as overwrought, xenophobic, and antipathetic to Hispanics. Brimelow's scholarship, he asserts, is "shoddy" and cluttered with stereotypes misleading statistics.

Section Four concludes with two articles from *Foreign Policy.* In the first, James M. Clad considers American immigration policy to be confused and in need of reform. He is particularly critical of the present levels of immigration, which he estimated has exceeded fifteen million people in the last eight years. The pace of immigration, he argues, must be slowed. In rebuttal, Jeffrey S. Passel and Michael Fix maintain that critics of immigration are guilty of many "misperceptions and misinterpretations of fact." While the total number of foreign-born persons in the U. S. today is at an all-time high, their share of the population is only half of what it was in the 1870–1920 period.

THE COMING IMMIGRATION DEBATE[1]

In the late 1940s, when the Marshall Plan was being debated in Congress, Arthur Vandenberg, presenting the plan on the floor of the Senate, summoned up a vision of "270,000,000 people of the stock which has largely made America." He insisted, "This vast friendly segment of the earth must not collapse. The iron curtain must not come to the rim of the Atlantic either by aggression or by default." Nearly fifty years later Peter Brimelow, an Englishman by birth and a senior editor of *Forbes* magazine, has summoned up another vision of danger to the common European-American stock. Comparing himself to the Thomas Paine of *Common Sense,* he warns that the survival of the American nation-state is in peril to a degree scarcely seen since revolutionary days. Unless radical corrective measures are quickly taken, he says, unchecked Third World immigration will overwhelm the United States—its culture, its economy, and its ethnic identity—within a matter of a few decades. European-Americans will be just one more minority group in a nation that few of today's Americans, whatever their ethnicity, would any longer recognize.

Brimelow's vision of Europe and the United States (and, in particular, Britain and the United States) as ethnic brethren may seem as dated as Vandenberg's in the multicultural America of today. But in the national debate on immigration that may well dominate the 1996 presidential campaign, Euro-American nationality could be championed as the American nationality par excellence (rather than by default) by a majority that has belatedly discovered it wants to remain a majority. For that campaign Peter Brimelow has written what may prove to be an indispensable book.

This is so in part because of the highly contentious form the book takes. Brimelow serves up one imagined debaters' duel after another, with the final thrust invariably delivered by the author's side. Consider, for example, the following:

You hear a lot about PhD immigrants working in California's Silicon

[1]Book review by Jack Miles, book columnist and editorial writer at the *Los Angeles Times,* from *Atlantic* 275:130–40 Ap '95. Copyright © 1995 by *Atlantic.* Reprinted with permission.

Valley computer complex. Just under 3 percent of recent immigrants had PhDs, as opposed to just over 1 percent of native-born Americans. But that's only, say, 30,000 immigrant PhDs a year. And have you heard that surveys show some 10 percent of Mexican illegal immigrants . . . were *totally illiterate in any language?*

You haven't? Oh.

Of his eristic method Brimelow writes,

> Part of the cultural diversity I bring to the United States from Britain is a certain (ahem) contempt for American debating technique. I can't help it. It's inbred.
> American competitive debaters are given their topics in advance and earnestly learn all the arguments by heart. But British competitive debaters are told their topics, and which side they must take, only at the last moment. They are expected to succeed by quickness of wit and whatever facts they can dredge (or make) up.

What Americans feel toward the English high style in debate is, I suspect, rather like what the English feel toward the clever French: we admire the biting humor, the hard brilliance, but we doubt the underlying substance, and we recoil in particular from the emphasis on wittily destroying an opponent rather than patiently and dialectically exposing all aspects of some important subject. This is why in the long run William F. Buckley Jr.'s faintly English accent and acid English wit have limited rather than enhanced the trust he enjoys even among his ideological allies. In these matters, for better and worse, America is Roundhead and plain, England Cavalier and fancy.

Ironically, however, Brimelow has produced a Cavalier briefing book well suited to the needs of Roundhead controversialists who, in the plodding American manner, will want to be prepared for anything the coming immigration debate may require of them. Brimelow calls the contending parties, with polemical panache, "immigration enthusiasts" and "patriots." Others have used the more neutral terms "admissionists" and "restrictionists." But either party may profitably imbibe this bottled brio. One side will be confirmed, the other forearmed.

Some of Brimelow's claims seem unproved, however intriguing—for example, his observation that America's ethnic groups are sorting themselves out by region.

> California . . . is being abandoned by lower-income whites in particular, exactly the group that would appear to be most vulnerable to competition from unskilled immigrants. Much of this white flight is flocking to the intermountain West, which seems likely to emerge as part of America's white heartland.
> Less noticed, minorities are polarizing too. Asians move to California's

Bay Area—they now make up 29.1 percent of San Francisco County—
and to the Los Angeles megalopolis, even if they originally settled in other
parts of the United States.

Brimelow might have added that some blacks are returning to
the South. Still, if it is difficult to maintain the character of even
an ethnic neighborhood in a highly mobile society, will it not be
all the more difficult to establish and maintain an entire ethnic
region?

A more serious issue, though amusing enough in Brimelow's
telling, is immigration reciprocity. Brimelow formally inquired
into the possibility of emigrating to several of the countries that
send the most immigrants to the United States, and shares with us
what he was told. Here are some of the opening sentences:

China: "China does not accept any immigrants. We have a
large enough population."

Mexico: "Unless you are hired by a Mexican company that
obtains a temporary work permit, or a retiree older than sixty-five
who can prove financial self-sufficiency, you must get a six-month
tourist visa *and apply in person to the Ministry of the Interior in Mexico City.*"

South Korea: "Korea does not accept immigrants."

Jamaica: "You cannot simply immigrate to Jamaica."

Egypt: "Egypt is not an immigrant country."

But if, as so many claim, immigrants contribute more to the
economy than they cost, Brimelow asks, why are these countries
not eager for immigration—particularly for a highly skilled, well-
capitalized immigrant like him? The size of the population should
have nothing to do with it.

One admissionist response might be that these countries
should indeed encourage immigration and would be economically better off if they did so. A likelier admissionist response
would be "America is different": these countries may rightly
claim that they are not nations of immigrants, but America has a
different tradition. Historically, however, as Brimelow effectively
shows, the United States has experienced intermittent rather than
continuous immigration. Twice in the past we have deliberately
interrupted the flow. We could do so again.

Should we? This is the central question of the book and of the
upcoming national debate. Before that question is asked, however, the mistaken belief that large-scale legal immigration to the
United States is a purely natural phenomenon should first be
corrected. Heavy immigration has not just happened. It has come

about through political decisions. Many Americans remember the
Civil Rights Act of 1964. Too few remember the Immigration and
Nationality Act Amendments of 1965. At the time, proponents of
the new law, which ended national quotas and introduced the
family-reunification principle, confidently predicted that it would
bring about neither any dramatic increase in immigration nor
any significant change in the ethnic makeup of the United States.
Had either change been predicted, the law would not have
passed.

Both changes, however, are now accomplished fact. In 1990,
Brimelow reports, a staggering 1.5 million *legal* immigrants were
admitted, of whom only eight percent came from Europe, including some en route from Asia or the Caribbean by way of Europe.
In 1960 the U.S. population was 88.6 percent white. By 1990 the
percentage of whites had dropped to 75.6, and the Bureau of the
Census forecasts a further drop, to 64 percent by 2020 and to 53
percent by 2050.

Without congressional action this would not have happened.
Do we want it to continue happening?

In other words: let's suppose that it would indeed be impolite to raise
the question of ethnic balance—if a shift were occurring due to the un-
aided efforts of one's fellow Americans, resulting in different birthrates
for different groups.

But how can it be impolite to mention it when the shift is due to the
arrival of unprecedented numbers of foreigners—arbitrarily and acciden-
tally selected by a government that specifically and repeatedly [in 1965]
denied it was doing any such thing?

If by decision or inaction this process continues, then America will indeed be different—not just different from what it has
been but different from every other nation in the world in its
radical openness to immigration. No other nation, as Brimelow's
queries about emigration make clear, permits immigration by the
hundreds of thousands annually on criteria no more compelling
than "family reunification." None would dream of countenancing
a tremendous demographic transformation for that reason alone.

If the United States chooses to make itself truly the great
exception, the implications are virtually endless, one of them being a potentially profound transformation of black-white relations, as "now, suddenly, there are new minorities, each with their
own grievances and attitudes—*quite possibly including a lack of guilt
about, and even hostility toward, blacks.*"

In this regard Brimelow may be saying more than he realizes.
Within living memory virtually all who immigrated to the United

States became citizens, and all who became citizens took on American history as their own. Numerous poems and stories have been written over the years about the comedy and poignancy of this process. But more-recent immigrants, by no means excluding immigrants from Europe, evince little enthusiasm for what Lincoln called the "unfinished work" of building a nation on "the proposition that all men are created equal." They hold or divest U.S. citizenship on the basis of tax-savings yield just as some native-born Americans have done. Their attitude bodes ill for the United States as other than a business arrangement and particularly ill for what Gunnar Myrdal called the "American dilemma" of race relations after slavery.

Perhaps a few Americans formally espouse the view that their country is not truly a nation but only a political system, a kind of inherited calculus for reconciling the interests of a group of nations (or ethnic groups, to use the domestic designation) occupying a single territory. But even if we wish the United States to be no more than that, can we get away with it? Can the American political system—the polity, the state—survive the demise of the American nation? The state has survived past peaks of immigration by relying on the nation to assimilate the immigrants culturally. But if the nation can no longer assimilate new groups because it has itself become no more than a group of unassimilated, contending cultures, how will the state survive a continuous heavy influx?

Assimilation itself has come into some disrepute. Proponents of multiculturalism want to preserve the immigrant cultures and even languages rather than see them absorbed by a host culture. Even the mutual assimilation or accommodation of native-born groups one to another, though it continues, is questioned. The melting pot, once celebrated, is now sometimes reviled. Other metaphors—the mosaic, the salad—are preferred. True, some foresee a less separatist, more mutually appreciative multiculturalism—a new cosmopolitanism, if you will—on the far side of multiculturalism as we now know it. But will the new cosmopolitanism mature soon enough to guarantee the minimum cultural coherence that political coherence requires?

If there is any question about that, and, more important, if there is a serious question about whether immigration confers any economic benefits whatsoever, shouldn't the United States sharply curtail immigration, just to be on the safe side, given the other risks and stresses that accompany it?

Unsurprisingly, Brimelow believes that there is indeed a serious question about whether immigration confers any economic benefits. Surprisingly, however, and perhaps prudently, he goes no further than this. He attends to no single topic at greater length than he does to economics, but he concludes that the economic case against the status quo in American immigration must be built into the cultural case against it. In the last paragraphs of the second of his two chapters on the economic consequences of immigration, he summarizes as follows:

It's a simple exercise in logic:

1. *Capitalism (and no doubt every other economic system) needs specific cultural prerequisites to function;*

2. *Immigration can alter the cultural patterns of a society.*

Therefore—

3. *Immigration can affect a society's ability to sustain capitalism.*

Let's leave the last word with [the economist] George Borjas . . . : *"The economic arguments for immigration simply aren't decisive,"* he says. "You have to make a political case—for example, does the U.S. have to take Mexican immigrants to provide a safety valve?"

Brimelow is a financial journalist and a political conservative. He knows perhaps better than many liberal journalists that conservatives are divided about the economic consequences of immigration. Robert Bartley, the editor of *The Wall Street Journal,* notoriously favors open borders. Last November, William Bennett and Jack Kemp, conservatives who had campaigned against California's Proposition 187, gave the endorsement of their organization, Empower America, to an "Immigration Index" produced by the conservative Center for the New American Community. The index purports to show that, as Kemp put it, "immigrants are a blessing, not a curse."

Brimelow sees more curse than blessing. He observes, for example, that most Third World immigrant-sending countries are without income-redistributing social welfare. Accordingly, the ablest, richest people in those countries have little reason to move to highly redistributionist Europe or the moderately redistributionist United States. By the same token, the European poor have reason to stay home and the Third World poor have reason to come here.

Arguing against the importance of imported labor at any level of skill, Brimelow points out that Japan's extraordinary economic development has come about without the benefit of immigration. In a population of 125 million Japan has perhaps 900,000 resident foreigners; in a population of 260 million the United States has 23.4 million. And rumors to the contrary notwithstanding, Japan is not about to change its policy. Here is the response Brimelow got to his inquiry about emigrating to Japan:

Anonymous Japanese Official. (*complete surprise and astonishment*) "Why do you want to emigrate to Japan? . . . There is no immigration to Japan. (*Asked if there aren't political refugees or asylum seekers*) There might be three people a year who become Japanese (*chuckles*). And even they don't stay long, they try to emigrate elsewhere, like the U.S."

The Japanese have achieved economic success without immigration secondarily because their high savings rate has assisted capital formation but primarily, Brimelow says, because technical innovation is more important than either capital or labor.

Brimelow implies, however, and surely he is right, that Japan's immigration policy is ultimately dictated by cultural rather than economic considerations. When immigration policy comes down to dollars and cents alone, policy formulation may be postponed indefinitely. Each side will have its economists, and each month will provide new numbers to be crunched. Borjas (to whom Brimelow's intellectual debt is enormous) is probably right: what politics has done, politics must decide either to undo or to continue doing.

Brimelow himself is blunt about the political course he would have the nation follow. Here are some of his recommendations:

• Double the size of the Border Patrol.

• "Urgently" increase the size of the Immigration and Naturalization Service.

• Institute a new Operation Wetback to expel illegal aliens.

• If necessary, establish a national identity card.

• Go beyond employer sanctions to the interdiction of money transfers by illegals to their home countries.

• Make it clear that there will never again be an amnesty for illegal immigrants.

• Discontinue immigration for the purposes of family reunification. If family reunification is permitted at all, confine it to the nuclear family.

• Move the INS from the Justice Department to the Labor Department, and make an immigration applicant's skills the criterion for admission.

• Institute an English-language requirement for immigrants.

• Ban immigration from countries that do not permit reciprocal immigration from the United States.

• Cut legal immigration from the current one million or more annually to 400,000 (the 1972 Rockefeller Commission recommendation), 350,000 (the 1981 Theodore Hesburgh Select Commission recommendation), or 300,000 (the recommendation of the Federation for American Immigration Reform), or to an annual quota set by the Labor Department in response to the perceived needs of the economy (the approach taken in Canada and Australia).

• Cut back such special categories as refugee and "asylee."

• See to it that no immigrant is eligible for preferential hiring, set-aside college admission, or other forms of affirmative action aimed at historically excluded groups.

• Replace the omnibus census category "Hispanic" with national-origin or racial classifications as appropriate.

• Consider repealing the citizenship-by-birth rule and lengthening the time of legal residence before naturalization to five or ten years "or even to fourteen years, as it was from 1798 to 1801."

I strongly agree with Brimelow that American immigration law needs to be reformed severely and quickly. And many of his proposals make good sense. However, his call for a new version of Operation Wetback—the hated federal program that forced a million illegal Mexican immigrants to return to their homeland in the 1950s—is worse than reckless. In a 40 percent Hispanic, heavily armed city like Los Angeles, the mass expulsion of illegal Mexican immigrants could not come about without a violent disruption of civic, economic, and even religious order, and probably not without provoking a major international incident. Such an operation could be implemented only at gunpoint, and it would be resisted the same way. Its announcement would be a virtual declaration of civil war.

Since the American Revolution was a civil war, this Tom Paine redux may know only too well what he is calling for. Returning to his hero in his closing pages, he writes,

> It is simply common sense that Americans have a legitimate interest in their country's racial balance. It is common sense that they have a right to insist that their government stop shifting it. *Indeed, it seems to me that they have a right to insist that it be shifted back.*

In that passage the first two sentences may pass muster as common sense; the last is pernicious nonsense.

Immigration as a political issue changed the course of the last gubernatorial election in California, the nation's most populous state. In the next three most populous states—New York, Texas, and Florida—the issue is only slightly less salient. Among them, these four states virtually guarantee that the immigration debate will play a central role in the next presidential election.

President Clinton and the new Republican leadership in Congress are proposing different, rapidly evolving versions of a "National 187," imitating the California citizens' initiative that seeks to deny most government services to illegal aliens. Taking a further large step toward militant restrictionism, the American Immigration Control Foundation, whose honorary advisory board is heavy with retired military men, is distributing a questionnaire that includes the following:

America cannot control its borders because the U.S. Border Patrol has only 4,000 officers. That's not nearly enough manpower to control the flood of three million illegals every year. Experts have proposed assigning 10,000 troops from military bases near our borders (out of a total armed services of nearly 2,000,000) to assist Border Patrol officers in stopping the invasion of illegals. *Do you favor such a proposal?*

Experts believe if Congress would assign as little as 2,000 military personnel who have been forced to retire early because of defense cuts, but who still want to serve our country, they could give tremendous assistance to our seriously undermanned Border Patrol. *If such legislation was introduced in Congress, would you favor passage of it?*

The Border Patrol itself would probably prefer to see the Armed Forces reduced slightly and its own forces enlarged. But the same huge California majorities that supported Proposition 187 would probably support the full militarization of the border if asked—particularly if the recent devaluation of the peso produces, as expected, a new flood of economic refugees from Mexico. But if such an armed force were to cross over from guarding the border to rounding up aliens for Brimelow's new Operation Wetback, I am confident that there would be armed resistance.

Has Brimelow completely forgotten the Rodney King riot? His suggestion that the proportions of the population be shifted back (*Back to just what?* one asks) strikes me as incendiary. I agree with him, as I have already said, that current American immigration law is worse than unwise. It can and must be revised, and the rate of immigration can and must be reduced. But even if, with luck, the further effects of a bad law can be checked, we have no real choice but to live with the effects to date of that law. And to do that we must create a national culture that does not define any large portion of the citizenry as American by sufferance.

Brimelow manages to combine fear-mongering and tear-jerking when he writes,

The U.S. government officially projects an ethnic revolution in America. Specifically, it expects that American whites will be on the point (53 percent) of becoming a minority by 2050.

My little son Alexander will be fifty-nine.

But little Alex and his kind already constitute only 75 percent of the population. And if the boy takes after his dad and lives in dusky New York rather than in that intermountain refuge for displaced palefaces which Brimelow sees taking shape, then Brimelow *fils* will belong to an ethnic minority, locally, long before 2050. How is he going to make his peace with that?

Not, I fear, with much help from Brimelow *père*, whose view of American culture from its very origins is almost truculently Anglocentric. The black proportion of the American population was greater at the time of the Revolutionary War (20 percent) than it is today. But Brimelow, who generally stresses the nation over the state, defines blacks out of the revolutionary nation because at the time they were defined out of the state. About the native population he has not a word to say. One may grant the unwisdom of swamping the current American population in new immigrants and yet insist that this nation is not now *and never has been* culturally as English as Brimelow wants to believe. The multicultural assignment, accordingly, is not one that this nation has taken on gratuitously. From the start we have had no choice about it.

Alexander, when he grows up, will have no choice about it either. It lies at the heart of the ongoing American nation-building enterprise. American (increasingly, even British) national identity is not a given. It is endlessly constructed. And it is the multiculturalists, with all their faults, who have taken this constructive enterprise in hand.

Writing in a splendid twenty-year retrospective issue of *Parnassus: Poetry in Review,* the poet Rita Dove offers a critical essay on the poet Derek Walcott under the title, borrowed from Walcott, "Either I'm Nobody, or I'm a Nation." The challenge that Walcott has faced, personally and artistically, is the challenge of mixed identity; but if a black man born as a British subject on a Caribbean island may be said to face the challenge of mixed identity in an intense form, none of the rest of us, and certainly not Alexander Brimelow, can hope to escape it.

Culturally speaking, the key deformation of the oppressed is their confinement in a merely private life. As regards the collective, public life, they are, to borrow from Ralph Ellison, invisible men and women. But an artist may set himself the nation-building task of embodying the invisible, private lives of the minority and so delivering them into the visible, public life of the majority. His goal, however, will be not just the incorporation of the minority but also the reincorporation of the majority. The challenge is as much intellectual as moral, and it is not mastered by sentimentality or self-indulgence. Dove quotes an early autobiographical Walcott poem in which the poet's surrogate "vows not to make his life 'public' '[u]ntil I have learnt to suffer / In accurate iambics.'" By keeping his vow, Walcott has revised and enlarged the Caribbean and the British identity alike.

Brimelow has little truck with any of this. Few economists do. Unfortunately, since he rests his case against continuing heavy immigration on cultural rather than economic considerations, the omission matters considerably. Brimelow is not entirely silent on this topic. He urges on his readers David Hackett Fischer's huge *Albion's Seed: Four British Folkways in America.* But a more revealing moment comes when he comments on the question of whether a million Zulus would assimilate to American culture more easily than a million Englishmen.

This question was one of Pat Buchanan's contributions to the 1992 presidential campaign. Addressing it, the *Wall Street Journal* columnist Paul Gigot wrote, "The Zulus . . . would probably work harder than the English." To Gigot, the line was clearly a moment of sardonic humor. But Brimelow fairly foams in rebuttal.

> It should not be necessary to explain that the legacy of Chaka, founder of the Zulu Empire, who among other exploits killed all his concubines' children, sometimes with his own hands, massacred some seven thousand of his own subjects to mark his mother's death, sliced open a hundred pregnant women to satisfy a fleeting interest in embryology, and ordered executions at whim daily until his assassination . . . is not that of Alfred the Great, let alone that of Elizabeth II or any civilized society.

One would think that Gigot had been denouncing the uxoricides of Henry VIII rather than chuckling over British work habits. The emotion in Brimelow's reaction suggests, I believe, that an insufficiently examined personal agenda has compromised the author's public agenda; and given the special intensity of this issue, I fear that this personal agenda will do the public agenda no good. I say this with regret, however, for the central legal reform to which Brimelow calls his adopted country is one that desperately needs to be made.

At his best, Peter Brimelow is an inspired controversialist, determined to storm the enemy's redoubt where it is strongest, not where it is weakest. At his worst, he manages to be sentimental and brutal at once, holding little Alexander aloft on every tenth page while proposing a new Operation Wetback that would tear hundreds of thousands of Mexican Alejandros and Alejandras from hearth and home. Most at ease arguing the economics of the matter, he has the courage to admit that the matter can have no economic resolution and the greater courage to step forward as an apologist for the received Euro-American culture.

I regret that, having thus brought the matter to a cultural point, he goes no further than he does in cultural analysis. But for all that, he makes a powerful—indeed, nearly overwhelming—case against the status quo. And if his book is at times uncomfortably personal, it is also painfully honest. Sometimes it takes a personal book to make a public debate finally and fully public. This could, just possibly, be one of those times.

CLOSING THE DOOR[2]

A few years ago I was present when a University of California vice president browbeat an unsuspecting undergraduate into silence. The offending student had innocently asked if California's emerging budget crisis was traceable to population pressures stemming in part from immigration. "No," the usually smooth but now ruffled administrator shot back, "there is no connection whatsoever between immigration and population growth in California, and linking the two smacks of bigotry and racism."

This exchange occurred well before Governor Pete Wilson and Proposition 187 transformed the immigration issue into a national political controversy. Today, not only would that student be less vulnerable to such treatment, he might well be brimming with confidence, particularly if he were armed and ready with arguments from *Alien Nation: Common Sense About America's Immigration Disaster,* a sassy but uneven anti-immigration polemic by Peter Brimelow.

Brimelow, a senior editor at both *National Review* and *Forbes,* and an immigrant (from England) to this country himself, has

[2]Book review by Peter Skerry, award-winning author and visiting fellow at The Brookings Institution, from *Commentary* 99:70–73 May '95. Copyright © 1995 by *Commentary.* Reprinted with permission.

been ringing alarm bells about immigration for several years. Indeed, an article he wrote in 1992 helped launch the current debate. In *Alien Nation,* Brimelow draws liberally on the work of his colleague, John O'Sullivan, *National Review*'s chief editor (another immigrant from England), who has argued that the United States is not the exception among nations that Americans like to believe it is; that Americans are bound together not only by devotion to a shared set of abstract principles but by the organic ties of language, history, and culture so important to other nations; and that immigration puts these ties under threat.

Brimelow marshals an impressive array of demographic and economic data to press this case, stressing in particular that today's immigrants differ significantly—for the worse—from those who came in earlier days. Thus, he presents evidence that over the past few decades the level of skills and education which immigrants bring to the United States has been in a steady decline. He also draws attention to the fact that in the same period the flow of immigrants has increased steadily from year to year independently of economic growth, whereas in the past immigration fluctuated with the cycles of the economy. Brimelow suggests that this decoupling can be attributed to the expansion of the American welfare state, which enables immigrants to remain even when jobs are scarce. The net effect of these trends, he concludes, is that immigration brings few if any economic benefits to the United States.

It is not, however, the economic drag caused by immigration that appears to trouble Brimelow most. Rather, it is the dramatic increase in the non-European share of the total immigrant mix. During the 1950's, he notes, 26 percent of legal immigrants came from Mexico and other Latin American countries. By the 1980's, that figure had grown to 30 percent, while the share of Asians coming as legal immigrants jumped from 6 to 45 percent.

As a consequence of this shift in composition, writes Brimelow, anyone riding the New York City subway or sitting in an Immigration and Naturalization Service waiting room will find himself "in an underworld that is not just teeming but is also almost entirely colored." He points with dismay to demographic projections indicating that one day in the next century, whites, who have always constituted the "specific ethnic core" of the "American nation," will be a numerical minority in the United States.

Brimelow would have it otherwise. He advocates policies that will result in fewer immigrants overall; and of those who are admitted, he wants more "who look like me." To this end, he favors limiting illegal immigration with such measures as: doubling the size of the U.S. Border Patrol; sealing the U.S.-Mexico border "with a fence, a ditch, and whatever other contrivances that old Yankee ingenuity finds appropriate"; reviving Operation Wetback, the controversial 1954 campaign that rooted out and summarily deported thousands of illegally resident Mexican nationals (along with a few Mexican-American citizens); and eliminating all public benefits to illegal immigrants, including public education, as now mandated by the Supreme Court and challenged by California's Proposition 187.

Brimelow also insists that there must be no more amnesties for illegal aliens, and he suggests that Americans "may eventually" have to carry national identification cards. Finally, he advocates repeal of the clause in the Fourteenth Amendment guaranteeing citizenship to anyone born on American soil (including the offspring of illegal aliens).

The proposals for dealing with legal immigration in *Alien Nation* are equally sweeping. Brimelow suggests we should entertain an "immediate temporary cutoff of all immigration." Short of that, he advocates cutting legal immigration by as much as two-thirds, and replacing the current criteria for admission—based primarily on family unification—with criteria based on skills. He would eliminate affirmative-action benefits for all immigrants, legal and illegal, and would also do away with special categories of immigrants like refugees, who should wait in line, he says, like everyone else.

How strong is Brimelow's case against immigration? And do his proposals for curtailing it make sense?

About some things Brimelow is certainly right. Larger numbers of low-skilled, poorly educated immigrants from Asia and Latin America are coming to the United States than ever before. A growing number of immigrants *are* relying on the welfare system. And immigration is placing real strains on American society, particularly in places like California where the debate's epicenter lies. But about much else, Brimelow is either wrong or, at best, half-right.

Thus, his discussion of the economic effects of immigration is one-sided and ignores evidence that contradicts his case. He pays virtually no attention, for example, to the many ways that labor performed by immigrants—as farm workers, janitors, maids, factory operatives, nurses, not to mention doctors and scientists—serves the economic interests of ordinary Americans. Of those professional economists who have examined the question, most do not share Brimelow's negative appraisal of the contribution immigration makes to the national balance-sheet.

As for Brimelow's warning that immigration is degrading the character of American society, the alarm bells he sounds on this score do not ring in harmony with the firm data we have on the pace at which assimilation—linguistic, cultural, and economic—is proceeding among most immigrant groups today. His argument is so broadbrush that a number of important details are obscured.

Thus, he lumps together Hispanics, whose progress is admittedly problematic, with Asians, who are generally doing quite well. He does not address the implications of the high rate of intermarriage between whites and "people of color." He refuses to take seriously the fact that a majority of Hispanics identify themselves racially as white, a category-blurring phenomenon he only grudgingly acknowledges. He also ignores abundant evidence that individualism, an important dimension of the national culture he seeks to protect, is thriving among immigrants today.

Even if Brimelow were to consider and somehow refute all of these objections, one would still be left wondering about his openly racialist vision of our society, which, ironically enough, has something in common with the position advanced by multi-culturalists and many immigrant leaders who see our country not as an imperfect melting pot, but as a nation of rival tribes.

Brimelow's policy proposals are also troublesome, not least because he never addresses, or even acknowledges, the monumental difficulties of realizing most of them, or the economic consequences of doing so. It is one thing, for example, to call for sealing our southern border, and quite another to reconcile that goal with the desire of American citizens to travel to and from Mexico with a minimum of disruption and delay. It is similarly doubtful that most Americans, much less Mexican-Americans, would tolerate anything like a revival of Operation Wetback with its round-ups and deportations. As for a national identification card, this is a proposal with some merit but, again, one that faces political opposition from both ends of the spectrum and is thus a long way from becoming law.

Though Brimelow's racial preoccupations are wrong-headed and his solutions unrealistic, reasonable people do have grounds to be concerned about the undesirable and long-ignored ways in which immigration has meshed with the welfare state and with such unfair social policies as affirmative action. Brimelow deserves much credit for getting discussion of these issues under way, even if immigration and the heterogeneity it brings are much more woven into the warp and woof of American society than he seems to understand or is ready to concede.

XENOPHOBIA FOR BEGINNERS[3]

Not so long ago, the literature of egregious bigotry was treated like pornography. You had to send for it by mail—from backwoods presses that advertised in the classified sections of conservative magazines—or frequent the political equivalent of dirty bookstores. Today, just walk into any Barnes & Noble. The Free Press set the precedent last fall with Charles Murray and Richard Herrnstein's *The Bell Curve,* which argued that blacks are genetically less intelligent than whites. Now comes Random House with Peter Brimelow's *Alien Nation,* another expression of intellectualized white rage that attempts to do for immigrants, and Hispanics in particular, what Murray did for blacks. Odds are it will enrage sensible folk, convince no one, and earn a small fortune.

Murray and Herrnstein were enough cowed by the taboo they were violating to bury their conclusions and couch them in the obscure argot of social science. Brimelow, a journalist at *Forbes* and a British immigrant himself, doesn't bother to mumble. The browning of America, he contends, is self-evidently a Bad Thing. To quote his peroration: "Any change in the racial balance must obviously be fraught with consequences for the survival and success of the American nation. It is simply common sense that Americans have a legitimate interest in their country's racial balance. It is common sense that they have a right to insist that their government stop shifting it. Indeed, it seems to me that they have a right to insist that it be shifted back."

Wow. Brimelow tries to inoculate himself by complaining in

[3]Article by Jacob Weisberg, contributor of *New York,* from *New York* 28:24, 26 Ap '95. Copyright © 1995 by K-III Magazine Corporation. All rights reserved. Reprinted with permission of *New York* Magazine.

advance about people who will seize upon this rhetoric to call him racist. It *is* regrettable to end conversations with name-calling. But what is racism if not an unreasoned objection to living alongside people who aren't the same race? And an unreasoned objection his is. Instead of offering arguments, Brimelow simply appeals to "common sense" (he fancies himself a latter-day Tom Paine) and postures about the sort of country his very white three-year-old son, portrayed on his father's knee on the back cover, will inherit.

But forget for a moment the book's in-your-face vileness and consider its evidence. To demonstrate that we're experiencing a catastrophic deluge, Brimelow resorts to statistical abuses that would make a high-school debater blush. His first distortion is a chart that shows immigration in absolute numbers. By including those who applied for legal status under the temporary amnesty of a few years ago, he succeeds in producing a recent "spike." But what matters is the number of newcomers relative to population. And that figure is quite low, something like one fifth what it was between 1900 and 1910. Even in absolute terms, the numbers are pretty unimpressive. In the early years of the century, when the population was about seventy-five million, legal immigration exceeded a million per annum; the population is now 260 million and immigration runs in the 800,000 range, including refugees. Desperate for some way to make the situation look terrifying, Brimelow points out that those born elsewhere now account for 37 percent of population growth. But this hardly testifies to a mass influx, since population growth overall has tapered off. A more meaningful statistic is the percentage of our population that is foreign-born. At less than 7 percent, that number is, once again, much lower than at many points in American history.

Though Brimelow seems truly alarmed by off-whiteness of all shades, it is Latinos in particular that drive him up a tree. About this "strange anti-nation inside the U.S.," as he calls them, Brimelow resurrects all the timeworn canards about immigrants: They're criminal, they bring diseases, they reject our culture, they refuse to learn English and assimilate, they take our jobs, they drain our resources, and so on and so forth. He might at least have made an effort to explain why the dire forecasts didn't prove true before but will now. Instead, he defends the "nativist" tradition. Among his self-described heroes are the Know Nothings, who he argues were not unreasonable in objecting to the arrival of Irish Catholics fleeing the potato famine.

One could painstakingly try to refute all of the current arguments against immigration, but most of them can't be found here. *Alien Nation,* which grew out of an article in *National Review* (a magazine edited by John O'Sullivan, another anti-immigrant immigrant Brit), is remarkable for its intellectual shoddiness. Sources cited in its footnotes include the least savory of anti-immigrant propaganda, and things like dust-jacket extracts. Brimelow makes his own points in ludicrous sound bites. After noting an estimate that immigrants generate an economic surplus of only $6 billion to $18 billion, while costing the government $16 billion (an estimate disputed by the vast majority of serious economists), he continues: "If immigration is indeed causing a net loss to the taxpayers of $16 billion . . . that means its economic effects are neutral. It's a wash!!! America is being transformed for— *nothing?* Yep. That's what it looks like." Well, nope, it doesn't (or *nope, it doesn't!!!,* as Brimelow would say).

When challenged at a recent Manhattan Institute lunch, Brimelow repeated a defense he makes ad nauseam throughout his book: He doesn't need to prove his case, because the burden of proof rests upon those who support immigration. It is they who need to demonstrate the benefits of changing America, not he who needs to defend keeping it the same. This is where Brimelow shows just how flawed his understanding of America really is. "The same" is immigration. Immigration, writes the historian Maldwyn Allen Jones, another, more enlightened Britisher, is "America's historic raison d'être . . . the most persistent and the most pervasive influence on her development." In fact, throughout American history, immigration has been restricted only intermittently.

Brimelow asserts that thanks to immigration, the U.S. is on the verge of turning into a cauldron of ethnic conflict on the order of Lebanon or Yugoslavia. Why? Because, he blithely contends, multicultural societies don't work. But America isn't a multicultural society. It's a melting pot with a tiny minority of radical separatists. The children of immigrants continue to learn English and assimilate despite the excesses of bilingual education, as they always have. I am not surprised that Brimelow fails to understand this. But I am amazed that Random House publisher Harry Evans (yet *another* anti-immigrant English immigrant) has gone out of his way to give these half-baked musings his personal endorsement.

None of this is to say that there aren't problems with the current system. Illegal immigration is an obvious one. The bias of the 1965 reform act, which skews the immigrant pool by giving heavy weight to distant family ties, is another. The result has been to favor a few ethnic groups, the largest of which is unskilled and poorly educated Mexicans, and to crowd out many nationalities whose immigrants can't enter because they don't have relatives here. Immigration is also unfair to states like California and Florida, which disproportionately attract newcomers. This is because the economic benefits of immigration flow to the federal government, while most of the costs accrue locally. In New York City, where the foreign-born population exceeds 25 percent, tax revenues generated by immigrants do not cover the cost of increased school enrollment, for instance. But all of these problems could be solved with a sound reform bill. We need to caulk the cracks along the border, downgrade the preference for non-immediate family, and come up with federal help for immigrant-swamped regions. It's not that complicated.

And there's one new admittedly xenophobic restriction I *would* support: an indefinite moratorium on right-wing Brits coming to tell us about threats to American values. As Archie Bunker might say, If you don't like it here, go back where you came from.

SLOWING THE WAVE[4]

In politics, as in life, one can either acquiesce in the inevitable or, like Canute commanding the tide to recede, be overwhelmed by it. The future of immigration into the United States may offer the same hard choice. We can either acknowledge, reluctantly, that immigration on the scale of the last three decades increasingly conflicts with other national priorities, or we can persist on our *laissez entrer* course and run a high risk of incurring a nasty nativist reaction to immigration. That sort of reaction would bring profound and unpleasant consequences for our society, our civil liberties, and, not least, our foreign relations.

[4]Article by James C. Clad, specialist in Asian affairs and former senior associate at the Carnegie Endowment, from *Foreign Policy* 95:139–50 Summer '94. Copyright © 1994 by The Carnegie Endowment for International Peace. Reprinted with permission.

The immigration debate is far from over despite its lower profile after some sensational events in 1993. Immigration is rising in stature as a foreign policy issue as well, commanding since 1993 an increasingly important if unpublicized place in U.S. bilateral ties with a range of countries, such as Belize, Brazil, China, Colombia, the Dominican Republic, El Salvador, Ghana, Guatemala, Haiti, Honduras, India, Jamaica, Mexico, Nigeria, Pakistan, Panama, the Philippines, Poland, Romania, and Russia. The 1993 controversies over illegal immigration led to new diplomacy—much of it little reported by the news media—to counter alien smuggling, strengthen the border with Mexico, harmonize migration abatement strategies with other Western countries and Japan, and tighten asylum procedures.

Officials in the State Department's proposed Bureau of Population, Refugees, and Migration accept that unwanted movement of people toward the United States will increasingly preoccupy our foreign relations. [With] . . . the September 1994 United Nations Conference on Population and Development . . . U.S. support for international programs that reduce Third World fertility and keep migrants at home may increase. Measures by the U.S. Immigration and Naturalization Service (INS) to deter migrants, including tougher penalties for airlines or other transporters of illegal immigrants, have begun to be noticed in African, Caribbean, East European, and Latin American countries; meanwhile, the INS is now looking at stronger sanctions, such as total authority for seizure of assets, to stem the flow.

In a world of vanishing barriers and unprecedented international mobility, the increasing desire of many Americans to roll up the welcome mat may seem contrary to the spirit of the times. But the question "how many immigrants?" must be answered. The era of global openness released tremendous new potential for migration to the West. Electorates in most Western countries are demanding more restrictive immigration policies linked to their countries' economic interests and core values.

In the United States, opponents of mass immigration cite reports that immigrants draw more from health and education than they contribute. A study by Rice University's Donald Huddle finds that immigrants cost the American government $40 billion annually. Other studies have linked low-skilled immigrants to weakened American global competitiveness. According to those studies, the flood of cheap, unskilled labor tends to lower investments in productivity improvements.

To be fair, many studies overstate their results, blaming immigration for economic shortcomings such as insufficient investment in capital goods. More important, the "dollars-and-cents" arguments miss a point that should be frankly acknowledged: Immigration is a cultural issue that raises serious questions about assimilation. Recent migrants appear to have less incentive to make a decisive break from their home countries. Fax machines, direct-dial telephones, next-day videos of home country entertainment and news, abundant foreign-language TV stations, cheap jet travel—all those nurture and reinforce an enclave mentality. The rapid transformation of immigrants into Americans, once touted as this country's unique achievement, no longer seems to happen so thoroughly or quickly. In this era of omnipresent telecommunication and affordable travel, the crucial psychological break with the home country need not occur: Migrants opt instead to establish a U.S. residence while staying connected, on a day-to-day basis, to their home countries.

Despite such anxieties, America's immigration debate remains grounded in inertia. Statue of Liberty symbolism and narrowly focused commercial interests favor the status quo. Many groups oppose restrictive immigration reform—including immigration lawyers mindful of future fees and libertarian advocates of open labor markets. Also opposed to reform are those wanting potential entry for specific national or religious groups and corporate farmers insisting on cheap field labor. Whatever their specific aims, these advocates mine a deep vein of guilt over past U.S. decisions to turn migrants away on racial grounds. They also capitalize on the myth of limitless American abundance.

Over the last four decades, pro-migrant sentiment has flowed from Cold War policies designed to induce people to flee communist countries. More recently, the INS issued directives, only partially observed in practice, granting asylum claims to any Chinese citizen able to reach the United States and voice opposition to China's one-child family planning policy. (Although some asylum claims ultimately have been rejected by the Board of Immigration Appeals, most claimants in the meantime have vanished into America's many Chinatowns.) Periodic INS and congressional open-door policies toward Russian Jews, Armenian Christians, Cubans, Vietnamese, and others have added to the pressure.

The major pro-migrant tilt in recent decades came after 1965 when, determined to jettison national and racial origin quotas once and for all, Congress inadvertently downgraded skill preferences in our immigration policy. It opened the borders instead to generously defined "family members" of U.S. residents, and that change led to "chain migration," which reinforced the enclave phenomenon. Meanwhile, difficulty in patrolling borders also allowed major flows of illegal immigrants.

What remains is a formidable inertia over a politically unsustainable status quo. Open-ended family reunification policies; deliberate confusion of refugees with economic migrants by members of Congress, public advocacy groups, and the media (all of whom refer to any asylum seeker as a "refugee"); and a porous southern border have pushed immigration to historic numerical highs. The legal influx during 1993 alone rose almost one million, 40 percent more than in 1987. More than eight million legal immigrants arrived between 1983 and 1991, with three-quarters of them going to just six states: California (35 percent), New York (14 percent), Texas (9.5 percent), Florida (7 percent), Illinois (5 percent), and New Jersey (4 percent). About twenty-five million foreign-born persons live in the United States today, up from fourteen million in 1980. Augmented by even moderate reckonings of illegal immigration into the United States, the net inward migrant flow may have exceeded fifteen million people during the last eight years. In 1989, the Census Bureau forecast a U.S. population of 300 million by 2050, but in 1993 it changed its mind. After factoring in high immigration rates, the estimate rose to 383 million.

The domestic reaction to immigration intensified in 1993 for two reasons. First, the weak economy focused popular discontent on immigrants seen as competing for scarce jobs. Second, sensational incidents involving illegal immigrants hit the headlines, most notably the World Trade Center bombing, carried out by Islamic extremists, the shooting of CIA employees by a Pakistani asylum applicant, and a number of incidents involving ships dumping thousands of Chinese economic migrants onto American shores.

Popular unease about immigration comes from a surprisingly wide band of opinion. The arguments range from demographic, environmental, and cultural concerns to broader if less articulate convictions that immigration does "more harm than good." During 1993, the latter reached an apogee in California, where polls showed that a majority of Orange County residents believed illegal immigration to be a "major problem." Other politically important areas in the next presidential election—Florida, Texas, and the eastern seaboard cities—also showed a similar unease. Misgivings surfaced as well among America's older minorities, particularly African and Hispanic Americans.

Cultural complaints against recent migrants have also gained ground. Whether prompted by raw prejudice or by legitimate concern over the future of assimilation, many believe that the United States shelters isolated immigrant communities with little affinity for the rest of the country. In this view, America's newest immigrants dwell in transplanted cocoons, temporary work stations insulated from surrounding society. Within such enclaves, home language, home customs, and (thanks to liberal family unification rules) plentiful faces from home sustain a sense of difference from mainstream American society.

Behind that sentiment lies a much more controversial issue: Many, perhaps most, Americans still see their nation as a European settler country, whose laws are an inheritance from England, whose language is (and should remain) English, whose institutions and public buildings find inspiration in Western classical norms, whose religion has Judeo-Christian roots, and whose greatness initially arose from the Protestant work ethic. Those beliefs may not (and should not) command the respect they once enjoyed, but to contemptuously dismiss their residual influence is to invite a very unpleasant reaction.

Other trends add to the unease. Increased attention to immigrant organized crime by the tabloid press also soured the national mood. Numerous stories, from credit card scams to drug smuggling, unfortunately give immigration and immigrants bad press. And on the demographic side, even moderate U.S. population scenarios sketch a world besieged by numbers, choked by Third World fecundity.

The Clinton administration responded to such fears in 1993 by reversing bureaucratic habits that treated migration as "low" rather than "high" politics. With few exceptions, the foreign policy establishment has long ignored migration. That practice changed after President Bill Clinton's July 27, 1993, policy pronouncement on illegal immigration. Meanwhile, in the Congress, simplistic posturing abated during 1993 with the convergence of liberal and conservative opinion. Senator Dianne Feinstein (D—California) warned of a "serious backlash against all immigrants, if strong and prudent federal policies to protect our border are not put in place."

Within Clinton's White House, opinion shifted toward preemptive steps against illegal migrants, on the basis that America's attitude toward migrants could quickly sour if distinctions between legal and illegal migration are not sharpened. Among conservatives, libertarian viewpoints (which once welcomed immigrants as a corrective mechanism in labor markets) were muted, while cultural conservatives advocated exclusionary or restrictive policies.

Many of the suggested reforms in immigration law could impinge heavily on America's foreign relations. Bills introduced in 1993 urged faster review of deportation orders, stricter asylum standards, and summary powers to evict aliens from ports-of-entry. A draft "Immigration Stabilization Act of 1993," introduced by Senator Harry Reid (D—Nevada), set an annual cap of 300,000 admissions per year and a ceiling of 50,000 refugees (in 1994, the Clinton administration sought 120,000 refugee admissions). Bills introduced by Reid and his colleagues in the Senate, and in the House of Representatives by members from California, Florida, Illinois, Maine, Michigan, Nevada, New York, and Texas, would also eliminate appeals by criminally convicted aliens, increase penalties for visa fraud, allow interdiction at sea of migrant smugglers, and prevent children born to illegal aliens within the United States from becoming U.S. citizens. None of those proposals is destined to become law; many of them perhaps need not. But they are harbingers of what will be a much more restrictive attitude toward immigration.

A Crowded and Restless World

The foreign policy issues raised by the immigration debate reflect various global "constants," including demographic, technological, and regional trends. Global demographic patterns, for example, guarantee steadily increased migratory pressure in the decades to come. The world's six billionth person will arrive in about five years, and the seven billionth will make his or her appearance in the new millennium's first decade. Even if disease and strife combine to raise mortality, and family planning programs push down fertility over the next fifty years, billions more people, predominantly from impoverished countries, are on the way. The U.N. Population Fund's *State of World Population 1993* report stated that the impact of mass migration across international boundaries is even greater than the figures suggest.

Deteriorating governance, local violence, and environmental

destruction will only add to migratory ambitions. Most discussions of global migration fail to catch the Third World mood of terrible yearning for a better life, and job-creating economic growth ultimately may be the only way to reduce migratory pressures. The initial phases of economic dynamism, however, usually spur migration rather than reduce it. The North American Free Trade Agreement (NAFTA) is designed to advance the Mexican economy, thereby benefitting the United States, but it will do little to slow Mexican migration; the dislocating effects of liberalized agricultural trade, a key NAFTA objective, may even accelerate it. A 1990 U.S. government commission studying international migration concluded that rapid economic growth weakens an individual's attachment to traditional ways, making it more likely that he or she will cross international borders.

If those demographic, migratory, and political trends hold fast, then there are many potential consequences for U.S. foreign policy. Some status quo analysts point fearfully to the closed-door 1920s, when Congress prohibited most immigrant categories following thirty years of influx from eastern and southern Europe. Even earlier, the 1882 Chinese Exclusion Act and the 1907 Japanese Exclusion Act preceded 1917 legislation declaring all of Asia a "barred zone." In 1924, the National Origins Act further designated Eurocentric immigration preferences.

While editorial comments abroad predict a recurrence of that starkly racist mood, the anti-immigration tide in the United States reflects more a reluctance to take in indefinite numbers of unskilled immigrants and less bias toward race or ethnicity. The exclusionary arguments are cultural and economic: maintenance of a common society, a better deal for America's older minorities, fiscal cost, and international economic competitiveness.

When and if tighter immigration quotas emerge, they should take an across-the-board approach. Clinton set the right tone in his June 1993 statement. "It is a commonplace of American life that immigrants have made our country great," he said, "but we also know that under the pressures that we face today we can't afford to lose control of our own borders, or to take on new financial burdens, at a time when we are not adequately providing for the jobs, the health care and the education of our own people."

Immediately after Clinton's announcement, American ambassadors delivered some pointed démarches to China, Taiwan, and Thailand, accusing officials there of cooperating with criminal syndicates to smuggle Chinese migrants into the United States. Belize, El Salvador, Guatemala, Haiti, and Pakistan also received warnings. That high-level concern about clandestine migration coincided with similar worries in Japan; in the twelve months ending in June 1993 alone, Japan's navy intercepted nine vessels carrying Chinese migrants headed for Japan and towed them back to China. After American pressure, Taiwan agreed in August 1993 to pay for the repatriation of mainland Chinese trying to slip into the United States via Guatemala after crossing the Pacific on Taiwanese-registered ships.

The assault on foreign complicity in alien smuggling was just one aspect of a broadening migration-related diplomacy. In September 1993, the United States and its European allies presented a draft migrant smuggling convention to the U.N. General Assembly. The draft convention places increased responsibilities on "out-migration" countries such as China and on such maritime flag-of-convenience countries as Taiwan, Honduras, and Panama.

Our most difficult immigration diplomacy will continue to be conducted with Mexico, the largest source of migrants to the United States. During the domestic American debates on immigration in 1986 and again in 1993, Mexico formally protested congressional and administration rhetoric aiming to reduce the migrant flow. A March 1994 INS report says that even "using extremely conservative estimates, . . . [from fiscal year 1990 to fiscal year 1992] no less than 67 percent of [Mexico's] total migration flow to the U.S. was comprised of illegal immigrants, and the illegal component may have comprised as much as 87 percent." The report "finds total migration from Mexico into the United States was at least 515,000, and may have been as high as 1,195,000."

The impact of immigration issues on foreign policy will center on combating runaway population growth. Thanks to our mythology of wide open spaces, we Americans fondly imagine we inhabit a different planet than the Europeans. Europe's population will increase by only fifteen million between 1990 and 2025 while North Africa's will soar by 132 million. But demographic disparities of similar magnitude will occur between the United States and parts of Latin America. Mexico and Guatemala's population will grow 170 percent and 235 percent, respectively, over the same period, according to U.N. projections. Clinton's increased funding for international population programs and the end of the freeze on funding for international family planning organizations are important first steps in reducing high birth-rates. Yet global population planning assistance amounts to just 1.4 percent of all aid, and the United States gives 40 percent of that total, its lowest share in a decade. The U.N. International Conference on Population and Development in Cairo in September would provide a good forum for renewed attention to population issues. The Clinton administration should use the conference to announce new fertility control programs and to boost global population planning aid. The United States can link population growth explicitly to migratory pressures, announcing that it seeks less of each.

Beyond that, serious border monitoring should receive more funding. In 1986, then president Ronald Reagan said that "future generations will be thankful for our efforts to humanely regain control of our borders" when he signed the Immigration Reform and Control Act (IRCA) into law. Pro-migrant lobbies say border barriers achieve nothing and are inhumane; yet some of the new technology—such as signal-processing radar and infrared imaging—is effective and the results of pre-screening and better fence barriers in Texas and California are encouraging.

Fines on air and sea carriers indifferent to passengers' documentation are another important but underenforced part of border control; Sweden, for example, puts offending ship captains or aircraft pilots into jail. Serious control means revoking landing rights the first time airline employees assist alien smugglers. It means stricter political asylum standards, and stopping the "presumptive asylum" tests accepted by previous administrations. Serious border monitoring means augmenting the tiny number (150) of INS political asylum examiners, who were overwhelmed by nearly 300,000 backlogged cases in 1993.

Americans cannot be anxious about global demographics and mass migration yet remain complacent about the anomaly of favored groups entering the country as "exceptions." We must stop using the migratory option as an inducement to leave, as we have done for Cubans, Russian Jews, and Vietnamese (but not Haitians). Nor should it become a diplomatic measuring stick to which we tie conditions. Those confused habits run deep. The Clinton administration's extension of MFN privileges to China in 1993 depended in part on China's permitting its people the freedom to migrate. Yet the same administration works feverishly behind the scenes to pressure Beijing to restrain Chinese from moving illegally to the United States. We must recognize as perverse our desire to win both a generalized freedom for anyone on the planet to migrate and our wish that far fewer people would head our way.

Americans may soon demand imposition of real, consistent immigration ceilings. "Despite a decade of so-called reforms, the United States' immigration system" remains "a patchwork of pork-barrel deals, contradictory rules, embarrassing errors and outright abuse," as the *San Jose Mercury News* noted in 1993. Our byzantine entry system creates a huge black market for phony documents, with entire industries devoted to producing them in places like Honduras, India, Mexico, the Philippines, Taiwan, and Thailand.

Immigration reform must reemphasize work skills as the primary criteria. In 1992, more than one-third of the 1.4 million legal immigrants entered under family sponsorship. As much as 10 percent gained legal residency via amnesties legislated in 1986. Immigrants winning political asylum accounted for another 7 percent (around 104,000) of the entrants. Yet those possessing needed skills—surgeons, nurses, technicians—numbered fewer than 50,000.

Americans now face a tough choice. Either we tighten migrant entry and reduce abuse of entry procedures, or we risk a backlash that could destroy our traditional welcome to skilled immigrants and individual victims of persecution even as it blocks unskilled migrants.

The contemporary immigration debate has many antecedents in our history. Illegal Chinese aliens were a major issue for organized labor during the last century; Chinese immigration became, as one historian put it, an "indispensable enemy." Yet as we reflect on historical parallels, let us also remember our historical cycles. From 1881 to 1920, 23.4 million immigrants arrived; from 1921 to 1965, a period of tighter restrictions, only 9.7 million entered, allowing time for the assimilation of the previous arrivals. Since 1965, the number of illegal and legal immigrants may be as high as thirty million, perhaps many more.

It is time once again to slow the pace. While immigrant yearnings may stand as true today as in the past, times have changed. The impetus for migration has risen in pace, frequency, and volume. The crushing momentum of world population growth is real. The technologies enabling easy, swift migration are real. The turmoil pushing people out of their countries is real. The cultural, social, and fiscal burdens of accepting them are real as well.

Ultimately, the hardest realization of all is that America cannot accept everyone who wishes to come here. In that hard fact lies the dilemma of today's immigration debate. The sheer number of the planet's potential migrants speaks for itself, and we cannot wait for the outcome of debates about whether "free markets" or "human inventiveness" can somehow feed an overcrowded world. The irony is that we need to act preemptively, and restrictively, in order to preserve our traditionally generous, assimilative stance toward genuine asylum seekers or persons with skills. In today's world migration can never be stopped altogether, but it can—and should—be slowed.

The United States has the sovereign right, if it constitutionally reflects the majority view, to exclude others from coming here. It is that simple; it is that awkward. The essence of sovereignty remains the power to exclude. America's confused good intentions, porous frontiers, and immigrant mystique still give a green light to the world beyond. New York's Statue of Liberty was never intended by her sculptor to be a standing invitation but rather, and far more significantly, to serve as a standing inspiration to a crowded world.

MYTHS ABOUT IMMIGRANTS[5]

In November 1990, President George Bush signed the Immigration Act of 1990, an expansive law that increased legal immigration by 40 percent. He declared that the law was "good for families, good for business, good for crime fighting, and good for America." In 1994, however, immigration has reemerged as a pivotal issue. It now defines political conflict over the basic values of American society—much like race, taxes, and crime—and evokes racial, cultural, and economic anxieties. Unfortunately, as the public debate intensifies, it is increasingly characterized by disagreement over facts as well as policy. The immigration issue, like other "wedge" issues, encourages rhetorical excess, often involving serious misperceptions and misinterpretations of historical fact and contemporary research. James Clad's article, ["Slowing the Wave"] . . . falls victim to much of the misinformation and misperceptions so common in the field of immigration today.

[5]Article by Jeffrey S. Passel, director of the Urban Institutes' Program for Research on Immigration Policy, and Michael Fix, director of the Institutes' Immigration Policy Program, from *Foreign Policy* 95:151–60 Summer '94. Copyright © 1994 by The Carnegie Endowment for International Peace. Reprinted with permission.

Agreement about facts does not imply agreement about policy, but a generally accepted factual base and framework is essential for rational assessment of policy alternatives.

The structure and goals of U.S. immigration policy are frequently misunderstood. U.S. immigration policy needs to be viewed as not one, but three fundamentally different sets of rules: those that govern legal immigration (mainly sponsored admission for family and work); those that govern humanitarian admissions (refugees and those granted asylum); and those that control illegal entry. The distinction is important because each category is governed by different legislation, involves different networks of bureaucracies, is guided by different goals, and results in immigrants with largely different characteristics.

The attention given to the failure to stop undocumented immigrants has led journalists, the public, and many politicians to conclude that U.S. immigration policy, as a whole, has failed. Our research and that of others indicates that this is not the case. However, the focus on undocumented immigration has blurred the "bright line" between legal and illegal policy and eroded the legitimacy of legal and humanitarian admissions.

The failure to recognize those distinctions also leads to the common misunderstanding that U.S. immigration policy is driven almost entirely by *economic* goals. In fact, legal immigration policy serves many goals. It is also intended to serve the important *social* goal of unifying families (principally of U.S. citizens) and the *cultural* goal of promoting diversity in the U.S. population and immigrant stream. Refugee policy is intended to serve the *moral* goal of promoting human rights. Most assessments of U.S. immigration policy do not acknowledge the power and value of noneconomic goals.

Finally, the number, characteristics, and adaptation of immigrants entering the United States as refugees, as legal immigrants, and as illegal immigrants all differ in important ways. The differences are seldom understood and often ignored in research and in policy debates.

Magnitude of Immigrant Flows

The composition of the immigrant population and flow are generally misperceived. The vast majority of immigrants in the United States are here with the country's express consent. Of the nearly twenty million immigrants counted in the 1990 census, only about 15 percent were here illegally. In fact, fully one-third of the immigrant population has made the effort to naturalize, swearing allegiance to the United States by becoming citizens. That figure is surprisingly high, representing about half of all immigrants who have lived in the country long enough to be eligible for citizenship. While the *number* of foreign-born persons in the United States is at an all-time high, the *share* of the population that is foreign-born—8 percent in 1990—is much lower than it was throughout the 1870–1920 period, when close to 15 percent of the total population was foreign-born.

The size and composition of the annual immigration flow is also often misinterpreted. Approximately 1.1 million immigrants arrive in the United States each year. About 700,000 are legal permanent residents, with family-based admissions accounting for almost three-quarters of the total. A large majority of the family immigrants are close relatives of U.S. citizens, not distant relatives of recently arrived aliens. Refugees and other humanitarian admissions add another 100,000–150,000 each year. Undocumented immigration contributes about 200,000–300,000 people annually, less than 30 percent of the immigrant flow.

Immigrant admissions remained relatively constant through the 1980s and then rose about 25 percent through fiscal year 1992 as a result of the 1990 act. That trend is consistently misinterpreted by the news media and the public because Immigration and Naturalization Service (INS) data on immigrants are unclear. The INS data on "immigrants" represent the number of persons becoming "permanent resident aliens." As a result of the Immigration Reform and Control Act of 1986 (IRCA), more than 2.7 million formerly illegal immigrants were granted legal status. That process involved becoming a "temporary resident alien" for several years before acquiring permanent resident alien status. Those several million individuals entered the country before 1985, with most arriving before 1982. However, they appear in INS data as "immigrants," beginning with small numbers in 1987 and peaking at more than 1.1 million in 1991. As a result, the official figures on "immigrants admitted" erroneously appear to have tripled between 1987 and 1991, followed by a 50 percent drop in 1992, the most recent year for which the INS has published a yearbook. The IRCA group masks the actual trend, which is a steady, incremental rise in admissions.

The amount of undocumented immigration is invariably overstated. The most informative measure of illegal immigration is growth in the population that enters and stays—200,000–300,000 a year. That figure, though not insignificant, is far below the more than one million stopped at the border each year; they are largely temporary labor migrants who are often apprehended multiple times, make multiple trips to the United States, and often leave the country uncounted and largely unnoticed.

The character of illegal immigration is also misunderstood, as it is associated almost wholly with Mexico. Although Mexicans represent the largest component of the illegal population, more than one-half of undocumented immigrants enter legally but overstay the duration of their temporary visas. Consequently, the undocumented population is more ethnically diverse than is commonly assumed (only about one-third is Mexican) and control measures will require more than improved enforcement and barriers along the U.S.-Mexican border.

Pace and Diversity of Immigration

One of the most striking features of contemporary immigration has been the rapid shift in the origins of immigrants, resulting largely from legislative changes in 1965. Europe, which accounted for two-thirds of legal immigrants in the 1950s, sent only 15 percent in the 1980s. The increase in Asian immigration has been the most dramatic, up from 6 percent in the 1950s to 45 percent in the 1980s. Latin America increased its share of legal immigrants to about 40 percent in the 1960s, but its share has not grown since then, although the absolute numbers have increased. Another indicator of the increased diversity is that the number of countries with at least 100,000 foreign-born residents in the United States grew from twenty in 1970 to twenty-seven in 1980 and forty-one in 1990 (data from censuses).

The force of immigration is also intensified by its pace. Almost one-half of immigrants in the United States today were not here a decade ago. By contrast, only 29 percent of the 1970 immigrant population had arrived in the previous decade. Because immigrants' incomes tend to rise with time in the United States, as does their knowledge of English and other dimensions of adaptation to their new country, the recency of arrival of today's immigrants fosters a misperception of their potential for integration into American society.

Characteristics of Immigrants

The shift in origins of immigrants has led to a broad perception that their "quality" has declined over the past several decades. Our research indicates that quality is related to legal status. Despite widespread belief to the contrary, when U.S. census data are disaggregated, they reveal that recent legal immigrants actually exceed natives on conventional measures of "quality." On the most conventionally used criterion, education, the credentials of *legal* immigrants—which are high to start with—actually increased during the 1980s. About one-third of the legal immigrants age twenty-five and over had college degrees, compared with only 20 percent of U.S. natives. Only one-quarter of the legal group had less than a high school diploma, a figure just marginally greater than that for the native population.

The educational credentials of people from countries that sent large numbers of *illegal immigrants* account for the perception of declining immigrant quality. Dramatically low numbers (less than 5 percent) have college degrees, while more than 75 percent are high school dropouts. The educational profile of *refugees* is intermediate.

An even better measure of "quality" may be household income. Recent legal immigrants have average household incomes that fall only 7 percent below those of natives. For those who arrived before 1980, both *legal* immigrant households and *refugee* households have average incomes that significantly exceed those of natives. Again, the recent refugees and immigrants from countries sending large numbers of illegals both have low incomes; they account for the perceived "low quality" of recent immigrants. The pattern of improving incomes with increased time in residence in the United States, together with the large percentage of newly arrived immigrants, suggests the need for any policy review to take a dynamic view of immigration, not a static one.

In addition to the scale of current immigration, its pace, and diversity, several other factors must be taken into account when assessing the impact on the United States.

Geographic Concentration

Unlike most other social issues in the United States, immigration exerts its most pronounced effects in only six states. About three-quarters of immigrants entering in the 1980s went to California (which received nearly four of every ten), New York, Texas, Florida, New Jersey and Illinois. In addition, immigration is an overwhelmingly urban phenomenon. More than 93 percent of immigrants settle in metropolitan areas versus only 73 percent of natives. The combination of geographic concentration and the general decline of urban institutions such as schools complicates the country's ability to integrate newcomers and distorts perceptions of immigrants' impacts.

Economic Impacts

Recent worries over the economic impact of immigrants have been exacerbated by the failure of the U.S. economy to expand employment between 1989 and 1992. During that period, when net job creation amounted to 250,000, several million new immigrants arrived. (In contrast, during 1986–1989 7.7 million jobs were added.) Of course, since 1992 the economy has grown rapidly and 1.7 million jobs were added in 1993 alone, so the view of immigration's effects may improve in the near future.

Our review of the economic literature indicates that despite claims that immigrants take the jobs of native workers, studies using aggregate statistics drawn from census data indicate that immigration had no meaningful job displacement effects. The studies also indicate that immigrants have only a small effect on wages, varying from place to place depending on the vitality of the local economy. In strong local economies, immigrants increase economic opportunities for natives; in weak ones, they have a small negative effect on the economic opportunities of low-skilled workers.

Those results may seem counterintuitive. However, many commentaries overlook the positive, but often indirect, benefits of immigration. Immigrants are slightly more likely than natives to be self-employed. Their businesses employ both natives and immigrants. Further, the incomes that immigrants earn, save, and spend ripple through the country's economy in ways that are only rarely credited to immigrants. According to the 1990 census, immigrants earned more than $285 billion in 1989, or about 8 percent of total income, almost exactly the same as immigrants' share of the total population.

Public Sector and Fiscal Impacts

Perhaps the most hotly contested question in current debates on U.S. immigration policy is whether immigrants use more in public services than they pay in taxes. The best recent research using a variety of data sources and modes of inquiry estimates that all immigrants arriving after 1970 pay a total of $70 billion in taxes to all levels of government, thereby generating $25–$30 billion more than they use in public services. That finding is sharply at odds with a number of seriously flawed studies done by groups advocating cuts in legal immigration or by governments seeking "reimbursement" for their expenditures. The impacts, however, vary considerably by legal status and level of government.

Immigrants represent a net fiscal plus. From a fiscal standpoint, most of the surplus accrues from legal immigrants; illegal immigrants seem to generate more expenses than revenues across all levels of government. The U.S. structure of fiscal federalism often obscures the positive aspects of immigration. Studies consistently find that immigrants represent a net gain to the federal government; that their impacts vary at the state level, depending on the structure of state services; and that immigrants, like natives, use more in services than they pay in taxes at the local level. That pattern of differing impact is exacerbated by geographic concentration of immigrants.

A particularly contentious area of fiscal impacts has been immigrants' use of public assistance. Here again, a full understanding requires distinguishing among immigrant groups on the basis of when they arrived in the country and what their legal status was at that time. In doing so, welfare use among immigrants is found to be concentrated among refugees to a degree that is largely unrecognized. Refugees, alone among immigrants, are eligible for benefits from the time they arrive in the country. The other group of immigrants with disproportionate use of welfare is elderly immigrants, who have come to the country at such advanced ages that they cannot accumulate sufficient work experience to qualify for Social Security benefits. Welfare use among nonrefugee, working-age immigrants (ages 15–64) is extremely low and, contrary to popular perception and some current research, falls well below that of natives. Welfare use among illegal immigrants seems undetectable.

Advantages of Immigration

Current calls for immigration reform emphasize two areas of concern: anxiety over the integration of immigrants into American society and immigrants' perceived negative economic impacts. Yet the weight of evidence indicates that the economic consequences of immigration are largely positive. Also, most immigrants are integrating socially and economically, and they are doing so without broad negative effects on their new communities. Some issues do require action. However, in considering reforms, it is essential to look beyond narrow economic calculations and keep in mind the multiple purposes of U.S. immigration policy, including social, cultural, and moral goals. Further, the different domains of policy—legal immigration, humanitarian admissions, and illegal immigration—each require their own policy responses. For example, reducing legal immigration and changing admission requirements for legal immigrants will not constrain humanitarian flows or illegal immigration. In fact, such actions may even have the opposite effect.

One conclusion supported by the evidence is that measures undertaken to control illegal immigration have been largely unsuccessful. Illegal immigrants are disproportionately poorly educated and low-skilled, tend to have low incomes, and generate net fiscal costs, particularly for local governments. Those findings, in turn, point to a need for altering the policies for controlling illegal immigration, not to a major overhaul of the country's legal admissions policy. Since the majority of illegal immigrants are not clandestine entrants crossing the southern border, but visa overstayers, increased border enforcement will be insufficient. One strategy might be to coordinate enforcement efforts for labor, tax, and immigration laws, focusing on the informal sector of the economy.

The concentration of immigrants in six states and in already-stressed urban areas raises questions about institutional capacity and fiscal fairness. The overall effects of immigrants, particularly legal ones, tend to be positive. In the short run, however, immigrants' adaptation to U.S. life may burden local governments since most revenues from immigrants (and natives) flow to the federal government, whereas the provision of services is the responsibility of local and state governments. That disparity has intensified over the past decade with cuts in the very few federal programs targeted on immigrants and their communities. Consequently, the issue of intergovernmental fiscal equity—an important aspect of immigrant policy—will require attention.

Several options are available. Distribution formulas for federal grant programs could be more responsive to the presence of immigrants. Another, perhaps complementary, approach could involve reimbursement of state and local costs associated with immigrants or even an immigrant block grant tied to the size of a specific population, such as recently arrived people who have limited English proficiency.

High levels of immigration give the United States underappreciated advantages in the world economy: America has a substantial population with familial, ethnic, and language ties to some of the most dynamic economies in the world. With increasing ease of communication and travel, those ties may be crucial for enabling American companies to become active and successful actors in an increasingly interrelated global market. It is time the immigration debate turns on facts rather than emotions. Erecting barriers (physical as well as legal) and pulling up the figurative drawbridge to protect American society are likely to dissipate those advantages that the United States has acquired over the last generation.

BIBLIOGRAPHY

An asterisk (*) preceding a reference indicates that the material or part of it has been reprinted in this compilation.

BOOKS AND PAMPHLETS

Aboud, John M. & Freeman, Richard B. Immigration, trade, and the labor market. University of Chicago Press. '91.

Adelman, Howard. Refugee policy. Center for Migration Studies. '91.

Aleinikoff, Thomas A. & Martin, David A. Immigration: process and policy. West. '91.

Anastos, Phillip & French, Chris. Illegal: seeking the American dream. Rizzoli. '91.

Anderson, Kelly C. Immigration. Lucent. '93.

Andryszewski, Tricia. Immigration: newcomers and their impact on the United States. Millbrook. '95.

Apraku, Kofi K. African émigrés in the United States. Praeger. '91.

Ardittis, Solon, ed. The politics of east-west migration. St. Martin. '94.

Ashabranner, Brent K. Still a nation of immigrants. Cobble Books. '93.

Auster, Lawrence. The path to national suicide: an essay on immigration and multiculturalism. American Immigration Control Foundation. '90.

Barbour, William. Illegal immigration. Greenhaven. '94.

Barken, Elliott Robert. Asian and Pacific Islander migration to the United States. Greenwood. '92.

Barry, Tom. Crossing the line: immigrants, economic integration, and drug enforcement on the U.S.-Mexican border. Resource Center. '94.

Borjas, George J. Friends or strangers: the impact of immigrants on the U.S. economy. Basic Books. '90.

Bottomly, Gillian. From another place: migration and the politics of culture. Cambridge University Press. '92.

Bouvier, Leon F. Peaceful invasion: immigration and changing America. Center for Immigration Studies. '91.

———— and Grant, Lindsey. How many Americans?: population, immigration, and the environment. Sierra Club. '94.

Briggs, Vernon M. Mass immigration and the national interest. M. E. Sharpe. '92.

Brimelow, Peter. Alien nation: common sense about America's immigration disaster. Random House. '95.

Brown, Judith & Foot, Rosemary. Migration: the Asian experience. St. Martin. '94.

Carrion, Ramon. U.S.A. immigration guide. Sphinx. '92.

Chambers, Iain. Migrancy, culture, identity. Routledge. '94.

Chermayeff, Ivan & Shapiro, Mary J. Ellis Island. Macmillan. '91.

Chierici, Rose-Marie. Demele: "making it": migration and adaptation among Haitian boat people in the United States. AMS. '91.

Chiswick, Barry R. Immigration, language, and ethnicity: Canada and the United States. AEI. '92.

Clinton, Bill. Accepting the immigration challenge: the president's report on immigration. U. S. Government Printing Office. '94.

Corcoran, Mary P. Irish illegals: transients between two societies. Greenwood. '93.

Cordosco, Francesco, ed. Dictionary of American immigrant history. Scarecrow. '90.

Cornelius, Wayne A., et al., eds. Controlling immigration. Stanford University Press. '94.

Cose, Ellis. A nation of strangers: prejudice, politics, and the populating of America. Morrow. '92.

Cox, Victor. The challenge of immigration. Enslow. '95.

Damaso, Ivan V. Immigration laws in America: what you need to know. World Legal Press. '92.

Daniels, Roger. Coming to America: a history of immigration and ethnicity in American life. HarperCollins. '90.

DaVanzo, Julie. Surveying immigrant communities. Rand. '94.

Davis, Marilyn P. Mexican voices/American dreams: an oral history of Mexican immigration to the U.S. Holt. '90.

Deatherage, Scott, ed. Immigration, new directions for the future. National Textbook. '94.

DeFreitas, Gregory. Inequality at work: Hispanics in the U.S. labor force. Oxford University Press. '91.

D'Innocenzo, Michael & Sirefman, Josef, eds. Immigration and ethnicity. Greenwood. '92.

Divine, Robert C. Immigration practice. Michie. '94.

Dublin, Thomas, ed. Immigrant voices: new lives in America, 1773–1986. University of Illinois Press. '93.

Dudley, William, ed. Immigration: opposing viewpoints. Greenhaven. '90.

Durand, Jorge & Massey, Douglas S. Miracles on the border: retablos of Mexican immigrants to the United States. University of Arizona Press. '95.

Eboling, Richard M. & Hornberger, Jacob G., eds. The case for free trade and open immigration. Future of Freedom Foundation. '95.

Edmonston, Barry & Passel, Jeffrey S., eds. Immigration and ethnicity: the integration of America's newest arrivals. Urban Institute Press. '94.

Fragomen, Austin T. & Bell, Steven C. Immigration fundamentals: a guide to law and practice. Practising Law Institute. '92.

Gabaccia, Donna R., ed. Seeking common ground: multidisciplinary studies of immigrant women in the United States. Praeger. '92.

Gardezi, Hassan. The political economy of international labour migration. Black Rose. '95.

Goldish, Meish. Immigration: how should it be controlled? 21st Century Books. '94.

Gorham, Robert F. Mitigating misery: an inquiry into the political and humanitarian aspects of U.S. and global refugee policy. University Press of America. '93.

Gould, W. & Findlay, Allan, eds. Population migration and the changing world order. Wiley. '94.

Grenquist, Barbara. Cubans (immigration to U.S.). Watts. '91.

Guitierrez, David. Walls and mirrors: Mexican Americans, Mexican immigrants, and the politics of ethnicity. University of California Press. '95.

Hauser, Pierre N. Illegal aliens. Chelsea. '90.

Heer, David M. Undocumented Mexicans in the United States. Cambridge University Press. '90.

Hing, Bill Ong. Making & remaking Asian America through immigration policy, 1850–1990. Stanford University Press. '93.

Hondagneu-Sotalo, Pierrette. Gendered transitions: Mexican experiences of immigration. University of California Press. '94.

James, Daniel. Illegal immigration: an unfolding crisis. University Press of America. '90.

Jasso, Guillermina & Rosenzweig, Mark. The new chosen people: immigrants in the United States. Russell Sage Foundation. '90.

Jones, Maldwyn A. American immigration. University of Chicago Press. '92.

Kilian, Pamela. Ellis Island: gateway to the American dream. Crescent. '91.

Kim, Hyung-Chan. A legal history of Asian Americans, 1790–1990. Greenwood. '94.

Krau, Edgar. The contradictory immigrant problem. P. Lang. '91.

Kraut, Alan M. Silent travelers: germs, genes, and the "immigrant menace." Basic Books. '94.

Lacey, Dan. The essential immigrant. Hippocrene Books. '90.

Lamphere, Louise, et al., eds. Newcomers in the workplace: immigrants and the restructuring of the U.S. economy. Temple University Press. '94.

Layard, Richard. East-west migration. MIT Press. '92.

Lee, Mary Paik. Quiet odyssey: a pioneer Korean woman in America. University of Washington Press. '90.

Legomsky, Stephen H. Immigration law and policy. Foundation Press. '92.

LeMay, Michael C. Anatomy of a public policy: the reform of contemporary American immigration law. Praeger. '94.

Long, Robert Emmet, ed. Immigration to the U.S. H. W. Wilson. '92.

Lopez, Antoinette Sedillo, ed. Latino employment, labor organizations, and immigration. Garland. '95.

Lutton, Wayne & Tanton, John. The immigration invasion. American Immigration Control Foundation. '94.

Mageli, Paul D. The immigrant experience: an annotated bibliography. Salem. '91.

Mayberry, Jodine. Eastern Europeans (immigration to U.S.). Watts. '91.

————. Koreans (immigration to U.S.). Watts. '91.

McClain, Charles. Chinese immigrants and American law. Garland. '94.

McGuire, William. Southeast Asians (immigration to U.S.). Watts. '91.

Mills, Nicolaus & Morrison, Toni, eds. Arguing immigration: the debate over the changing face of America. Simon & Schuster. '94.

Monto, Alexander. The roots of Mexican labor migration. Praeger. '94.

Moody, Suzanna & Wurl, Joel, eds. The immigration history research center: a guide to collections. Greenwood. '91.

Muller, Thomas. Immigrants and the American city. New York University Press. '93.

Nelson, Brent A. America balkanized: immigration's challenge to government. American Immigration Control Foundation. '94.

New York State Legislature. Senate. Committee on cities. Our teeming shore: a legislative report on the impact of U.S. immigration policy on New York State. New York State Legislature. '94.

O'Connor, Karen. Dan Thuy's new life in America. Lerner. '92.

Ong, Paul M., et al., eds. The new Asian immigration in Los Angeles. Temple University Press. '94.

Pachon, Harry & Desipio, Louis. New America by choice: political perspectives of Latino immigrants. Westview. '94.

Pencak, William, et al., eds. Immigration to New York. Associated University Presses. '91.

Portes, Alejandro & Rumbaut, Rubin. Immigrant America: a portrait. University of California Press. '90.

Pozzetta, George E., ed. Contemporary immigration and American society. Garland. '91.

————. Education and the immigrant. Garland. '91.

————. Ethnicity and gender: the immigrant woman. Garland. '91.

————. Folklore, culture, and the immigrant mind. Garland. '91.

————. The immigrant religious experience. Garland. '91.

————. Immigrant family patterns. Garland. '91.

————. Immigrant institutions: the organization of immigrant life. Garland. '91.

————. Immigrant radicals: the view from the left. Garland. '91.

_____. Immigrants on the land: agriculture, rural life, and small towns. Garland. '91.

_____. Nativism, discrimination, and images of immigrants. Garland. '91.

_____. Politics and the immigrant. Garland. '91.

_____. Themes in immigrant history. Garland. '91.

_____. The work experience: labor, class, and immigrant enterprize. Garland. '91.

Price Waterhouse. Foreign nationals in the United States. Price Waterhouse. '95.

Purcell, L. Edward. Immigration. Oryx Press. '95.

Reimers, David M. Still the golden door: the third world comes to America. Columbia University Press. '92.

Rivera, Mario A. Decision and structure: U.S. refugee policy in the Mariel crisis. University Press of America. '91.

Rowland, Robert C. United States policy on immigration. National Textbook. '94.

Rutledge, Paul. The Vietnam experience in America. Indiana University Press. '92.

Sandler, Martin W. Immigrants. HarperCollins. '95.

Settles, Barbara H., et al., eds. Families on the move: migration, immigration, emigration, and mobility. Haworth. '94.

Siegel, Martha S. The insider's guide to successful U.S. immigration. Harper. '92.

Siems, Larry, ed. Between the lines: letters between undocumented Mexican and Central American immigrants and their families and friends. Ecco Press. '92.

Simon, Ritz J. & Alexander, Susan H. The ambivalent welcome: print media, public opinion, and immigration. Praeger. '93.

Skeldon, Ronald, ed. Reluctant exiles? Migration from Hong Kong and the new overseas Chinese. M. E. Sharpe. '94.

Sorenson, Elaine. Immigrant categories and the U.S. job market. Urban Institute Press. '92.

Spencer, Sarah, ed. Strangers and citizens: a positive approach to migrants and refugees. Rivers Oram Press. '94.

Stave, Bruce M., et al. From the old country: an oral history of European migration to America. Macmillan. '94.

Takaki, Ronald & Stefoff, Rebecca. Ethnic islands: the emergence of urban Chinese America. Chelsea. '94.

Tifft, Wilton S. Ellis Island. Contemporary Books. '90.

Tomaso, Lydio F., ed. National Legal Conference on immigration and refugee policy. Center for Migration Studies. '93.

Ueda, Reed. Postwar immigrant America. St. Martin. '94.

Walch, Timothy, ed. Immigrant America: European ethnicity in the United States. Garland. '94.

Weissbrodt, David S. Immigration law and procedure in a nutshell. West. '92.

Yang, Philip Q. Post–1965 immigration to the United States. Praeger. '95.

Yoon, In-Jin. The social origins of Korean immigration to the United States from 1965 to the present. East-West Center. '93.

Youssef, Nadia. The demographies of immigration: a socio-demographic profile of the foreign-born population in New York State. Center for Migration Studies. '92.

Zhou-Min. Chinatown: the socioeconomic potential of an urban enclave. Temple University Press. '92.

ADDITIONAL PERIODICAL ARTICLES WITH ABSTRACTS

For those who wish to read more widely on the subject of immigration, this section contains abstracts of additional articles that bear on the topic. Readers, who require a comprehensive list of materials, are advised to consult the *Reader's Guide to Periodical Literature* and other Wilson indexes.

Defending the immigrant. George M. Anderson, *America* 170:17–19 Je 4–11 '94

Thousands of poor illegal immigrants whose only crime is to have attempted to enter and remain in the U.S. have difficulty obtaining legal representation in exclusion or deportation proceedings. Poor immigrants, unlike poor American citizens, have no constitutional right to free legal assistance. Crowded and isolated Immigration and Naturalization Service (INS) detention facilities make it difficult for foreign nationals in detention to contact legal representatives, and inaccuracies in lists of free or low-cost legal services often make such resources virtually useless. Language difficulties further complicate the availability of representation. Moreover, the number of low-cost, voluntary legal services is too small for the increasing number of immigrants in need. Finally, the INS often pressures immigrants to waive what few legal rights they have.

Life in the 90's. Terry Golway, *America* 172:6 Ap 22 '95

Peter Brimelow's new book, *Alien Nation,* contains absurd immigration-bashing arguments. Brimelow argues that America must close its borders to avoid being overrun with unskilled, violent, uneducated, service-demanding, and job-stealing hordes of immigrants. *Alien Nation,* however, sees nothing wrong with immigrants such as the white, Anglo-Saxon, Australian-born media magnate Rupert Murdoch, whose tabloids and Fox Television Network ensure that U.S. culture continues its downward spiral. Brimelow, who ironically is an immigrant from Britain, is attempting to impose his immigrant-wary British values on U.S. society.

Almost tasting trade. Gail DeGeorge, *Business Week* 32–3 S 19 '94

Even as images from Cuba's refugee crisis flood newspapers and TV screens, many American companies are exploring how doing business with the island nation could eventually affect their bottom lines. Despite an apparent stalemate over immigration issues and U.S. insistence that its thirty-two-year-old trade embargo not be discussed until Cuba takes clear steps to implement political and economic reforms, some firms are making tentative plans to trade and, eventually, invest there. Moreover, various American executives have ignored travel restrictions and visited the island for a first-hand look. However, despite their interest in an easing of U.S. policy toward Cuba, the corporate will does not exist to force the issue of trade with Cuba publicly. Most businesses remain unwilling to speak out against the embargo for fear of angering some factions of the Cuban-American community. Prospects for U.S. biotechnology, entertainment, and oil investment in Cuba are examined.

Who picks up the tab for aliens? Catherine Yang, *Business Week* 34 Mr 28 '94

Heavily burdened states are threatening to bring lawsuits against the federal government over the issue of immigration. On March 14, Florida governor Lawton Chiles repeated his vow to bring suit against Washington, demanding compensation for the nearly $1 billion annual cost of providing benefits to illegal immigrants. Governors in Arizona, California, and Texas are contemplating similar action.

Immigration debate divides Christians. John Zipperer, *Christianity Today* 39:42–3 F 6 '95

Disagreements over immigration policy are creating sharp conflicts among Christians in California following passage of Proposition 187, a measure that curtails government services for illegal immigrants. Despite opposition from many political and religious leaders, nearly 60 percent of the electorate favored Proposition 187. Supporters of the measure were part of a historic backlash against ineffective federal efforts to secure U.S. borders and the high cost to local government of providing health care and education services to millions of illegal residents. With the passage of the measure, Latino Christians, their churches, and other communities of color are now finding themselves the target of hostility toward new immigrants in America.

Immigrants and family values. Francis Fukuyama, *Commentary* 95:26–32 My '93

Some right-wing Republicans view third-world immigration as a threat to the traditional Anglo-American culture, but these people are deeply mistaken about the real sources of cultural breakdown. Immigrants from such places as Asia, Mexico, and Cuba are often characterized by a strong work ethic and a powerful commitment to family. The real threat is not that they will undermine the traditional culture but that they will themselves be corrupted by the antitraditional ideology of America's well-established white elite. This liberal elite is also responsible for the multicultural ideology that overpowers the assimilationist impulses of rank-and-file immigrants and undermines the idea of a common American culture.

Reform or resentment? *Commonweal* 122:3–4 Ja 13 '95

As the new Congress begins making what it promises will be radical social policy changes, it is to be hoped that its members will be able to distinguish between reform and resentment. Children and immigrants, who have no voice in Congress, are particularly vulnerable to the politics of resentment. The article assesses measures to crack down on illegal immigration and to create orphanages for poor children born to unmarried teen mothers.

Illegal child labor comes back. Brian Dumaine, *Fortune* 127:86–8+ Ap 5 '93

Child labor is on the rise again in the U.S. Government statistics have shown a marked rise in child labor law violations over the past 10 years, and a number of prominent recent cases have drawn attention to new problems: In many states, small fly-by-night candy distributors are hiring young children to sell boxes of candy in strange neighborhoods late at night without supervision; in New York City and Los Angeles, immigrant children are working in dangerous garment industry sweatshops; and in California, Texas, and south Florida, young children work with their parents as migrant farmers. The Labor Department, which recently fined Burger King $500,000 for child labor violations, is now investigating the Food Lion supermarket chain for hundreds of possible safety violations. A surge in immigration and a decline in middle-class family incomes are to blame for the increasing incidence of child labor. A sidebar discusses the effects of work on children's education.

Why we are losing the immigration game. George J. Borjas, *Fortune* 128:114+ O 18 '93

Part of a special section presenting excerpts from Fortune Encyclopedia of Economics. The U.S. is running behind in a worldwide contest to attract skilled workers. Immigrant workers compete with U.S. workers for jobs, but their entrance into the U.S. slightly increases the income of U.S. citizens overall. Unskilled immigrants consume more from the welfare system than they contribute to the economy, whereas skilled immigrants are an asset to the economy. Other host countries, notably Australia and Canada, consider such factors as education and occupation when allocating visas. The U.S. is being harmed by its failure to apply such measures.

Cuban gold. David Corn, *The Nation* 259:333–4 O 3 '94

The recent Cuba crisis might have been averted if President Clinton had approved a 1993 National Security Council initiative aimed at shutting down TV Marti, which broadcasts anti-Castro propaganda to Cuba in violation of international conventions, and loosening the embargo against Cuba. Instead, when Cubans started pouring into Florida, Clinton tightened the embargo, and Americans found it more difficult to visit or send money to family in Cuba or to travel there for educational purposes. Now, in spite of the apparent resolution of the immigration crisis, these bans remain. With even conservatives calling for a reconsideration of the embargo, Clinton has abundant political cover for reappraising his Cuba policy but seems unwilling to risk the wrath of the politically powerful Cuban-American right.

Five myths about immigration. David Cole, *The Nation* 259:410+ O 17 '94

The writer presents statistics and arguments to debunk five common myths about immigration: That America is being overrun with immigrants, that immigrants take jobs from U.S. citizens, that immigrants are a drain on society's resources, that aliens refuse to assimilate and are thus undermining America's cultural and political unity, and that noncitizen immigrants are not entitled to constitutional rights.

Know the flow. George J. Borjas, *National Review* 47:44–50 Ap 17 '95

Before any serious discussion can take place on the subject of immigration reform, it is necessary to dispel a number of myths about the economic impact of immigrants. Americans mistakenly believe that immigrants do well in the labor market, that they use welfare less than natives do, that they pay their way in the welfare state, that they do not hurt the earnings of native workers, that they are likely to be successful entrepreneurs, that the melting pot works quickly, that Americans gain a lot from immigration, that immigration is not very high now by historical standards, and that refugees and illegal aliens are the source of the immigration problem. All of these statements can be shown to be false.

Nationhood: an American activity. John O'Sullivan, *National Review* 46:36–45 F 21 '94

Part of a special section on multiculturalism. The true cultural expression of America is not a patchwork quilt of cultures distinct from each other, as multiculturalists claim, but a broader common culture that celebrates the achievements of different ethnic groups as part of a common history in a commonly understood language. The answer to the question "What is an American?" is clear to any foreigner and to the majority of Americans themselves. Only the political class and the intelligentsia seem to be mystified by the obvious. The writer discusses the idea of American nationhood as defined by such thinkers as Emerson and Tocqueville, the cultural heritage that early America inherited from the British, the challenge to this heritage posed by the rise of multiculturalism, and the multiculturalist argument that the high level of immigration to the U.S. requires a wholesale re-making of American culture.

A move to curb immigrant visas? David Warner, *Nation's Business* 82:65–6 F '94

The U.S. Labor Department's proposed restrictions on H-1B visas would make it more difficult for companies to hire certain highly qualified employees from abroad. The visas are designed to allow U.S. companies to hire foreign professionals for up to six years. Public furor over immigration, especially illegal immigration, in the midst of a slow-growing economy has put pressure on the Clinton administration to tighten restrictions. According to recent surveys, U.S. citizens believe that immigrants take jobs from them and use a disproportionate share of social services. There have also been charges that companies use visas to hire immigrants willing to work well below the prevailing wage—and below the wage a U.S. worker would accept. Discussed are the restrictions that have been proposed for H-1B visas, as well as for permanent business visas known as E-B visas, and measures introduced in Congress to reduce the number of legal immigration visas.

Don't panic. *The New Republic* 211:7 N 21 '94

California's Proposition 187 uses illegal immigrants as a scapegoat. Proposition 187 would deny illegal immigrants in California social services such as educational and medical benefits, even though a 1982 Supreme Court ruling found that illegal aliens are entitled to these services. If the proposition passes, teachers and nurses would be required to check the status of anyone they suspect is illegal and report violators to the Immigration and Naturalization Service, and students who are citizens would have to turn in their illegal parents, making for disastrous social policy. As many as 300,000 children could become homeless, and most illegals would probably forgo even basic medical service, such as immunizations, rather than risk deportation.

The closing door. Nathan Glazer, *The New Republic* 209:15–18+ D 27 '93

A variety of ethical dilemmas are posed by U.S. immigration policies. In light of the current debate over immigration, Americans must consider how many immigrants should be admitted, which nations and races should receive preference, and how immigration policies should be enforced. The writer traces American immigration policies and reforms from 1924 to the present and discusses the ability of America to assimilate immigrants, the economic approach to immigration policy, the current restrictionist movement, and possible responses to illegal immigration.

A questionable proposition. Andrew Murr, *Newsweek* 124:29 O 31 '94

Two nationally prominent Republicans—former housing secretary Jack Kemp and former education secretary William Bennett—have incensed California Republicans by attacking the Proposition 187 illegal immigration measure. California Gov. Pete Wilson, a Republican, has gained political strength by leading the campaign for Proposition 187, which promises—falsely, according to opponents—to save billions in tax dollars by restricting government aid to the state's estimated 1.7 million illegal aliens. In a joint statement against the measure, Kemp and Bennett attacked it as "pernicious," un-American, and potentially damaging, both to the GOP and to race relations. The statement has given an opportunity to nervous Democrats, including California Senator Dianne Feinstein, who opposes Proposition 187 and is in a tough re-election race. Still, the proposition's backers have succeeded in putting immigration on the national political agenda.

Why not deport these guys? David A. Kaplan, *Newsweek* 123:66 My 2 '94

Law enforcement officials are incensed that, in some states, criminal aliens, illegal or documented, can remain in the United States after serving their prison terms. Aliens can take advantage of due-process rights, particularly if they have green cards, families, or have been in the country for more than seven years. Alien felons also benefit from the fact that some state corrections officials and federal immigration officials do not communicate with each other. Criminal aliens typically must complete their prison sentences before becoming deportable; when an alien is about to be released, however, the Immigration and Naturalization Service (INS) may not know about the release, or if it does, may not be able to complete the months of deportation proceedings in time.

Hispanic population outnumbers blacks in four major cities as demographics shift. Sam Roberts, *New York Times* 34 O 9 '94

The Hispanic population now outnumbers blacks in Los Angeles, Houston, Phoenix, and San Antonio and is poised to overtake blacks in New York as immigration has surged and Hispanic birth rates have outpaced those of other groups. Analysts say the rise in the Hispanic population, which could be reflected in the nation as a whole within fifteen years, could have enormous political, social, and economic implications.

We have your number. Peter Cassidy, *The Progressive* 58:28–9 D '94

In response to mounting national concern over illegal immigration, the U.S. Commission on Immigration Reform has proposed establishing a Federal employment-eligibility database to discourage the hiring of illegals. The idea was warmly received by the media and many members of Congress but not by minority-rights and civil-liberties groups. Any such system would necessarily require the creation of a national ID card that could become a tool of State-sponsored control or harassment of minorities. Agencies like the Internal Revenue Service, the National Security Agency, and others engaged in law enforcement or espionage would be the ultimate beneficiaries of a national identity authentication system.

No fruits, no shirts, no service: the real-world consequences of closed borders. Glenn Garvin, *Reason* 26:18–26 Ap '95

Americans across the political spectrum hold the deluded view that immigrants steal jobs, use up natural resources, and dilute the culture. In fact, the American economy needs immigrants. Rather than taking jobs from Americans, many immigrants do work that Americans would refuse. Their labor in agriculture, child care, the garment industry, and other sectors would simply not be done—at least, not in the United States—if immigrants were not here. Immigrants have also played a crucial role in the success of American high-tech industries.

Alienable rights. Margaret B. Carlson, *Time* 144:39 O 31 '94

California's Proposition 187 is misguided. The measure aims to deny public health care and education access to the state's illegal immigrants. Prominent Republicans William Bennett and Jack Kemp have come out against Prop 187, saying that it is a nativist measure that appeals to the angry and won't fix the problem of illegal immigration. Moreover, most studies of Latino immigrants show that they have a strong work ethic, tight-knit families, and a low use of public services. Nevertheless, polls show that 59 percent of likely voters favor Prop 187.

Dangerous tides. Christopher John Farley, *Time* 145:56–7 Ap 10 '95

Increasingly, the Dominican Republic is the departure point for illegal immigrants making their way to the United States. The chief industry in dozens of coastal Dominican towns is illegal immigration, with refugees arriving from Latin America, Eastern Europe, the Middle East, and even China and Japan. They crowd into makeshift boats for the 110-mile trip to the U.S. commonwealth of Puerto Rico, where they can easily board a flight to New York City. The voyage is a brutal, shoddy affair organized by small-time thugs, condoned by bribe-taking public officials, and executed by approximately one hundred boat captains who live along the Dominican coast. To avoid detection, the boats set a course through a treacherous stretch of sea in the Mona straits, which separate the Dominican Republic and Puerto Rico.

Protecting U.S. borders against illegal immigration. *U.S. Department of State Dispatch* 4:561–5 Ag 9 '93

An overview of the Clinton administration's proposed plan to curtail illegal immigration into the United States. In remarks made on July 27, 1993, on the occasion of the announcement of the Clinton administration's proposed immigration policy, President Clinton, Vice-President Gore, and Attorney General Reno discuss the benefits of the proposed policy. A fact sheet released by the Office of the Press Secretary describes how the administration's initiatives regarding illegal immigration—to prevent illegal entry into the United States, remove and deport illegal aliens and alien felons expeditiously, and strengthen criminal penalties and investigatory authorities—will be implemented. Another fact sheet details the reforms contained within the president's proposed Expedited Exclusion and Alien Smuggling Enhanced Penalties Act of 1993.

A new line on Cuba. Linda S. Robinson, and Tim Zimmermann, *U.S. News & World Report* 118:47+ My 15 '95

Under a new immigration accord negotiated between Cuba and the United States, nearly all of the 21,000 Cuban refugees who have been detained at the U.S. naval base at Guantanamo Bay will be permitted to come to the U.S. The accord stipulates, however, that from now on, illegal immigrants will be returned to the island. The reversal of a thirty-six-year policy has enraged politically powerful Cuban-American leaders in Miami who claim that President Clinton is going soft on Castro, a charge supported by the administration's critics in Congress. A bill sponsored by Sen. Jesse Helms would deny visas to foreigners involved with expropriated property in Cuba, ban sugar and other imports from countries that buy Cuban sugar, and commit the U.S. government to defending property claims of Cubans who fled after the 1959 revolution. The administration, which sent Congress a six-page list of objections to Helms's bill, is trying to pressure Castro while attempting to foster change.

Coming to America. Brian Duffy, *U.S. News & World Report* 114:26–9+ Je 21 '93

A cover story examines illegal immigration in the U.S. More than nearly any other ethnic group, Chinese are crossing the nation's borders in droves through illegal smuggling operations. Once they arrive, many labor as indentured servants for years to pay the outrageous fees charged by smugglers. Under a system known as "credit ticket," a person wishing to leave China for America will make a down payment on the price of passage; the balance is to be paid from wages earned in the U.S. Prices and percentages vary, but can run into the tens of thousands of dollars. Discussed are the U.S.'s efforts to stem the tide of Chinese immigrants, the reasons why their numbers are expected to grow, the grip held by the smugglers over the immigrants, and the grounding of the Golden Venture, a ship carrying Chinese immigrants.

Lifestyle 2000: new enterprise and cultural diversity. Jerry Feigen, *USA Today* 121:66–7 Mr '93

U.S. history has proven that the diversity and creativity of the people who have emigrated here have driven the country's economic engine and will continue to do so into the next century. The business prospects of blacks, women, and Hispanics—who more recently have begun to exert their influence—have grown, just as the fortunes of such groups as Jews, the Irish, and Italians did.

Between 1982 and 1987, according to Commerce Department data, the number of black businesses with paid employees grew 87 percent, those owned by Hispanics grew 111 percent, and those owned by women grew 98 percent. Furthermore, cultural diversity will increase into the 21st century as black and Hispanic populations grow. The history of U.S. immigration since 1790 is described, and questions that will be faced by the U.S. next century are listed.

Losing control of immigration. *The Wilson Quarterly* 18:121–2 Aut '94

Illegal immigration is a highly charged issue in the United States. According to official estimates, some 3.5 million illegal aliens now live in the United States, and 200,000 to 300,000 more are arriving each year. Easy immigration has many supporters, including those who see it as an American tradition, free-market conservatives, employers who use unskilled workers, and liberal activists. Nonetheless, many Americans are frustrated over the tide of illegal immigration and the government's inability to stop it. Moreover, the distinction between legal and illegal immigration seems to be blurring. Articles in the Summer 1994 issue of the American Experiment, the Fall 1993 issue of Dissent, the July 1994 issue of the Annals of the American Academy of Political and Social Science, the Spring 1994 issue of Polity, and the Summer 1994 issue of the Responsive Community discuss illegal immigration.

As California goes . . . . Richard C. Carlson, *World Monitor* 6:20–3 My '93

Because of its worldwide influence, the social and economic problems facing California are matters of interest to non-Californians. California is

America's most populous state and has the eighth-largest economy in the world. Currently, however, it is experiencing major budget deficit problems, peace dividend job losses, tax stress, technology competition, immigration problems, and self-doubt. In the midst of the worst recession in twenty-two years, California had a budget gap last year that was larger than the entire budgets of all but three other U.S. states. The culturally diverse state also seems to be dividing into two societies, 1 prosperous, the other miserable. These problems are due, in part, to the state's soaring population growth rate—more than 500,000 per year—which, in turn, is mainly attributable to a large influx of immigrants and high birth rates, mostly among Hispanic immigrants. The article discusses the outlook for California's social and economic ills.